Preface

Today, there are countless religions and philosophies in the world, yet people still do not know where humanity came from or where they go. Are there philosophies and religions that can answer to those questions? Now is the time to rethink the aim of e role of religion. In this work, I could find amazing secrets about new heaven, the Victor in the Bible while I studied about the Victor who emits the hidden manna, and neohumans' culture. Now is the time when we dump the wrong view of God, salvation, the Savior that was made by extremely human and ignorant knowledge, religiously blind faith and idol about heaven, reexamine the definition and ultimate aim of religion, need discussions between religious bodies about their religious defunctionalization, and joint researches between new religions. Recently, Korean new religions often insist immortality, which is considered as a foolish thought to the existing religions and new religions with more than 50 years' history that lost the role and function of religion. However, the insistence of eternal life gives hope to modern people who live in well -being era, makes people realize the essence of humanity, is one step ahead than the exiting religions that are fading, have no vision, and are blind and irrational. Therefore, they are worth studying. Also they surface as a new paradigm that is systematic enough to be unparalleled with the existing religions, try to accomplish the words of the Scriptures, the will of heaven, and the aim of religion, and lead the world new religions. Due to advanced science and medicine, a lot of the equipment and ways of extending life-span approach to realizing humanity' s hope and dream. Furthermore, the development of scientific technique and biotechnology is going to realize humanity's dream variously, the immortality of NRMs of Korea is more persuasive and surface as interest of people comparing to the view of afterlife 'going heaven after death' of the existing religions. Regrettably, thanks to the existing religions' insane teaching and salvation theory, though death is the most important assignment to overcome, to study death is treated valueless. No matter how long the existing religions are, being under the work of death, they do not avoid responsibility for diluting and cranking down humanity's challenge and endeavor to overcome death. A lot of new religions, the alternative of existing religions, were formed in the commercialization and secularization of the big exiting religions that lost the original aim and the hope of religion are not beyond the frame of the existing religions, made humanity accept death naturally, though death is the enemy of humanity. Modern people who are in the era of Well-Being and Well-Dying put their Accent not 'on solving the problem 'die or not die', but on 'well'. Further, recently, meaningless 'Death Academy' appears, glorifies death, and insists that Well-Being and Well-Dying are beautiful and stylish. The phenomenon shows that there was no religion, science, and philosophy in the world to save people. That is, the reason that the insistence of religious immortality is treated distortedly, does not win sympathy, and is considered as surrounding religions is because the existing religions did not answer to the problems of death and life of humanity. That is, they lost their roles and functions as religion. Therefore, eternal life in NRMs of Korea is ignored as primitive religions. More regrettably, as the Korean existing religions that are tamed by western civilization, are not beyond the limit of western religions and philosophies become a standard to determine authenticity or cult, and drive Korean new religions to cults. In these bad situations, the wave of Korean new movements religious recovered their vigor, are dreaming the Idea World, and are predicted as a new wind of the world new religious movements. In fact, if religion neither overcome death nor lead the world of eternal light, it cannot be religion. From the Victor in the Bible who overcame death, there was neither the work of true religion nor philosophy and science. The existing religions which did not suggest the way of realizing immortality lost their roles. So they became an obstacle of the era of neohumans, awaken scholars insist that religion is useless. To understand the religious culture and the new paradigm of Korean new religious movements, people should ask essential questions about death and life and seek the answers. The insistences of NRMs of Korea, 'Physical eternal life' and 'one can be reborn as the Holy Spirit' are biblical, scientific and reasonable. Therefore, they are not blamed and tabooed ones. Rather it should be considered that they are the fruit of new new religious movement that the Victor suggests the answers to the questions of death and eternal life. I think they need a modest scholarly attitude to research the neohumans culture which solves the problems that existing religions could not. I found in the process of research that the subject that leads the Korean new new religious movements is not humanity, but the Victor in the Bible. That is, the religious movement is the unprecedented work of the Holy Spirit that the Victor leads directly. It can be explained as the last fruit of Korean new religious movement, a practical campaign of neohumans' culture's saving life and 'the One Body Philosophy' that makes all humanity one. It is a new hope of all mankind, the end of the religion by humanity, is the last step of the world new religions, and the revolutions of religion by the Holy Spirit of the Savior.

Contents

Preface

CHAPTER I. The Korean New Religious Movements
  1. The Beginning and Development of Korean New Religious Movements
  2. The 4 Unique Characters
  3. Nicknames of Korean New Religions
  4. The Role and Future of Korean New Religions

Chapter II. The New View of Afterlife & the Secret of New Heaven
  1. New Values & the New View of Being and Death of the Victory Altar
  2. The Secret of New Heaven & the Advent of Heaven's Man
  3. New Doctrine of the Victory Altar by the Tongsijeok Samse Deungmyeong

CHAPTER III. The Ultimate Aim of NRMs in Korea &
"The Law of Liberty" of the New Era
  1. The Ultimate Aim of Korean New Religions ß
  2. What are the new rules of the new world?
  3. "The Law of Liberty" as New Commandments

CHAPTER IV. The Hidden Manna of New Heaven & New Paradigm of NRMs
  1. A Study on the Secret of the Hidden Manna, GamRo-HaeIn(甘露海印)
  2. The New Theory of Immortality through the Principle of Blood

CHAPTER V. The New Method of NRMs & New Public Philosophy
  1. The New Method of New Religion Research
  2. What is the Han-moum Philosophy?

CHAPTER Ⅵ. The Hidden Secrets of the Victor & the Final Issue of NRMs
　　1.The Hidden Secrets of the Victor in the Bible
　　2. The Authority & Qualifications of the Victor
　　3.The Hidden Victor & the Secret of "The Lost Tribe"
　　4.The New Interpretations of Bible by the Victor
　　5.The New Culture by Neohumans & The Final Issue of NRMs

Closing

CHAPTER I
The Korean New Religious Movements

By knowing Tao's pedigree of Korean new religion connected with the beginning Donghak of SuWoon and the process of spirit's work by God, people can predict the future of Korean new religion and the direction of the world new religion. In this work, I went to Taiwan to participate in CESNUR, 2011, as a futurist who studied the world prophetic books and the world new religious movements for decades; I said in its abstract, by studying Korean new religions, people can understand all religions of the world, their religious movements and their future. Because a lot of world religions flew in Korea, Korea can be expressed as a religious department store or a religious market and forms multi-religious multi-cultural societies. As all the religions have been integrated, fused, coexisted, and developed, it is a foreshadowing that the will of heaven will be realized centering Korea. But few scholars know the fact. Furthermore, I will reveal that by studying the Victory Altar and Korean new new religions, people can see 'the culture of immortality', 'hidden manna', 'the sealed secret in the Bible and the advent of the Victor clearly. Like I suggested the Korean religious situation in CESNUR, 2011, as the religious phenomenon that is happening in Korea influences the society and culture directly, by studying and understanding the Korean new

---

★ I edited and curtailed my paper that was submitted to Korean New Religious Academy in Journal 24 volume, in 2011 and to reedit my papers that were submitted to the CESNUR, in Taiwan 2011, in Moroco 2012, in Sweden 2013.

religious movements, people can predict the future of all humanity of the world. Because the Victor is raising 300 righteous men to recreate an eternal world, which is full of the light of life. Also due to the open proclamation of the Victor's 5 public covenants and the Law of Liberty to establish new heaven, people started to admit the predictions of Tagore and the common insistence of Korean new religionists, "Korea will be the parents' country of all humanity of the world, the immortal world will be established in Korea".

1.The Beginning and Development of Korean New Religious Movements

Korean new religion means a new religious movement and group that came out the creation of Donghak in 1860. Following the influx of Confucianism, Buddhism, Taoism, and Christianity into the existing ancient God leading religion (神敎), Korean new religious movement became another factor that brought about change in Korean religious history. It is an opening of multi- religions that the traditional religion is mixed and coexists with foreign religions. Korean New Religion is composed of 14 religions; by their happening time, it is divided into their former part, which their religions were created, and their latter part, which a lot of sects were broken off. The former part of Korean New Religion appeared in the turbulent era of modern times, contributed to the modernization of Korea by leading the new education and the new female movement. Also, it helped the Korean independence army actively at home and abroad to achieve Korean independence from Japan during the Japanese colonial era. However, in their latter part, they did not accustom to the rapidly changing era, each sect was seriously divided. So their congregation and functions shrunk. Now, there are 14 religions, which have been divided into 300 sects. Some have the possibility to be developed. While the others is falling down its power. While Buddhism and Christianity are main, the status of Korean new religions is minor. However, among Korean new religions, some new Christianity grew rapidly enough to influence the politics and economy of Korea due to the power of politicians. The characteristic and aim of Korean New Religion is building the Utopia. It promises a big one world, a kingdom of 1000 years meaning the real paradise. I insist that building the Utopia is possible by the advent of the Messiah, who will establish the Utopia, the thought of integrating all religions as one thought (the thought of whole one), and the posterior big change to open a new era. I think it is realized not by waiting for the time but when a big wisdom based in the truth, detailed plans and capability to make a welfare society are fulfilled. The advent of the Victor and the Korean new religious movement in the Victory Altar, where the Savior fosters neohumans for building the Utopia, become a starting point to open a new era. So it becomes hope to a lot of scholars, ascetics, and the people who trace the truth. I referred a thesis titled, "The Utopia that Is Revealed in Korean New Religions" written by Lee Gyeong Woo, a legendary person in the field of Korean New Religions research, in the International Academy Neohumans Culture Journal Vol 2. I will use NRMs of Korea to express Korean new religious movement in the body of this thesis.

1)The meaning and history of NRMs of Korea

The history of Korean new religion started in the middle of 19th century when Angel Choi Je Woo, the creator of Donghak appeared; is about 150 years. Passing through modern times' turbulent era, Japanese dark colony, and the era of innovation after independence, the Korean new religions greatly influenced Korean contemporary history. Especially, NRMs of Korea became bases of independent movements, led in resistance to save Korea. However, the perception about Korean new religions is negative. This is a problem in themselves, but their weak congregation and low social awareness did not attract people's interest. Also the academia and media which focus on only existing religions becomes a factor. Thus the Korean new religions still remain surroundings of the religious world and academia. However they have a unique phenomenon. The meaning and final aim of NRMs of Korea are for all humanity to become one and to build the paradise to live happily forever. But its real worth was not revealed. Today, in multi-religion's era, Korean new religions hold a large majority. Also, unlike existing religions, Korean new religions have future-oriented consciousness and promising thoughts and cultures. So it is very meaningful to see as they are. Now in the body, I will discuss the various names of Korean new religions, their history spanning 150 years, their common features, their ultimate aim, the building of the Utopia, and how the Korean new religions will develop.

2)The process of the creating of NRMs of Korea

Korean new religious movements have 153 years of history starting with the creating of Donghak in1860. During that period, 17 religions, and 500 groups were created. Today, 14 religions and 300 groups are active. Dividing them before and after the independence from the Japanese occupation, Donghak system (동학계), Namhak system (남학계), Jeongyeok system (정역계), Jeungsan system (증산계), Dnagun system (단군계), Ganksedo system (각세도계), Gengjeongyoudo system (갱정유도

계), Meulbeop system (물법계), new Buddhism, new Confucianism, new Christianity, new foreign system, Moo system, general religion system were created. After the independence, Ilgwando system and United sindo system were created. Among them Namghak system, new Confucianism, and United system perished.

The NRMs of Korea before the Independence

The advent of new religions is roughly created when an existing order collapses and a new order is made. Modern times when new religions were created are those times. Periodically, when Choseon dynasty collapsed, a new government was not established, and Korean people lost their country. Socially, there were illogical systems such as social discrimination, the predominance of man over woman, oppression and exploitation. Religiously, the existing religions like Christianity and Buddhism lost their roles and could not become a prop for Koreans. Like that, when all things collapsed, civilians wondered, Korean new religion planted a new hopeful philosophy to Koreans suggesting a new order. Therefore, the advent of Korean new religions was inevitable; it was the demand of times. The main system of new religions came about before the Independence, by regional groups, Donghak was made in Gyeongsang province, Jeongyeok in Chungcheong province, Jeungsan in Jeolla province, Dae religion of Dangun system in Seoul, Gaksedo in Hanghae, Gangjeongyoudo in Jeolla province, Meulbop in Jeju. Geugangdaedo of general religion system was created in Gangwon province, One Buddhism in Jeolla province, and Youngju religion in Gyeonggi province. Like that the creation of Korean new religions spread all over the country. Yeongju religion was made in Gyeongi province and spread all over the country. Donghak that is the starting of Korean new religion was created by Choi Je Woo in 1860. After attainment of nirvana through answering to the questions of angel, he told his enlightenment, "learning is Donghak, Tao is heaven Tao." At that time, it was called Donghak, it was called Donghak Cheondo(heaven Tao) religion by later generations.

Korean new religions after the Independence

Before the Independence, it is a period of the creator of Korean new religion, after the independence, it is that of faction. The direct line congregation or collateral line that connected creators' religious tradition were split and showed jumbling while the third generation lasts. The Korean new religions before the Independence gave hope and comfort to the people who lost a sense of their direction, were frustrated in the turbulent period of modern times and the dark age of Japanese occupation, through new thoughts. They suggested ethical virtues such as human right, social justice, peace for mankind, diligence, abstinence, human love, public goodness, and win-win, developed independence movements to save their country. They showed the aspect of function quite. However, after the independence, they did not enter the contemporary times because the state of period was changed completely. The politics, economy, and society grew rapidly. They were unprepared to adapt to the changing society, and fell behind. Furthermore, impoverished existing religions thrived again. Christianity grew rapidly; the Korean new religions had no place. So they became minors. Meanwhile, some groups that hardened their foundation and produced competent people silently and some groups which some genius appeared and modified their doctrines into ones one step ahead in the process of sects' separation showed their competence, acted as much as Christianity. Please refer the classification of their system in Journal 『Neohumans Culture』, volume 2, 76~86page

2. The Features of NRMs of Korea, Unique Character

1) The Creation opening again post-heaven(Gyeobeok)

The great opening again post-heaven indicates the era of neo-humans which harmonize with science material civilization and ethics moral civilization. Especially, liberty and equality of humanity, peace, and welfare should be guaranteed. At that time, God and humanity will become one, the earth and heaven will become one, in-yang will become one, and people will be reborn as neutral. Male and female are equal, the era of posterior is 坤運, frontier female will be more than male. Gang Jeung San predicted "at the posterior era, transcendent female will be more than transcendent male". The rate is 9 females to one male. In fact, the numbers of female religious sect leaders are growing. Before the independence, there were 30 female religious sect leaders, after the independence, that number has grown to 120. The first female religious sect leader is Go Pan Lye.

2) The Thought of Maitreya and Messiah

The thought of Maitreya and Messiah is that the Maitreya Buddha that Buddhism and new Buddhism serve as their Buddha will come in Korea. The thought of the Savior or Messiah is revealed in new Christianity. The thought is based on the recording of Revelations and Isaiah, the phrases,' the end of the earth, the corner of the Far East'. However, each sect is not biblical; they interpret the revelation as Korean traditional thought. Cheon boo religion(Jeondokwna)called Pak Tae Sun the righteous man, the olive tree, the spiritual mother, and the Victor. Dongbang religion calls No Gwan Gong a mission man, Ilyecheonbu (이례천부) calls Illyesinmyeong(이례신명) a mission man at the end of times, Jangmak(tent) castle calls Yoo Jae Lyeol a young servant. And Sincheondohak research center(신천도학연구소) calls Sindongsoo the Second coming lord, the judge, and the second son of God. Segyeiljoo pyeonghwagook(세계일주평화국) calls Yangdojeon Jeongdoryeong, God church calls AnSanghong the Holy Spirit God, Heaven Evangelical church(천국복음회) calls Goo In Hoi the second coming Jesus, Palyoungsan prayer house(팔영산기도원) calls Jeon Byeong do Jehovah, Juhwaninsindoaecheonboo spirit love religion(주환인신도애천부성령애교) calls Jang ByeongMan the son of God, Jehovah, Seil church(여호와 세일교회) calls Lee Yoo Seong the substitute of God, Seoul center church(서울중앙교회) calls Kim Hwa Bok, the last servant at the end of times, and Stop babel mission(스톱바벨선교회) calls Choi Dae Gwang the servant at the end of times. Although they do not have a complete personality, they became sect leaders, Messiahs, and the Maitreya by their mysterious competence or revelations, the number of being called the Messiah or the Savior are around 3000.

3) The Thought of Unifying all religion into one(統宗合一思想)

The thought of unifying all religions into one is one that makes all religions one, is one that makes all religions the religion of the truth, and is the thought and movement that unifies all things. The representative religious movement is 'the One Body Philosophy' of the Victory Altar. Korean new religions mostly insist their doctrines are the succession or completion of the

Fairy Tao, the traditional Korean Tao. The Fairy Tao is the mental soil and heart of Koreans, the foundation of Korean culture. The thoughts of Confucianism, Buddhism, and Taoism were already melted in it according to the Nanglang secret letters of Choi Chi Won. Before Confucianism, Buddhism, and Taoism came to Korea, the Fairy Tao already taught their key points. Between the Fairy Tao and Korean new religions, there was a long time interval such as the period of the three statuses, unified Silla, Goryeo dynasty, and Chosen dynasty, Confucianism, Buddhism, and Taoism filled the interval. Therefore, when Korean new religions occurred, people accepted unifying Confucianism, Buddhism, and Taoism as one in their doctrines, not combining the thoughts of alien religions (Confucianism, Buddhism, and Taoism)but hugging them in succeeding or completing the Fairy Tao. So Confucianism, Buddhism, and Taoism are in the doctrines of Korean new religions, but they take partial role and functions. Such the thought of unifying all religion into one is the common feature of Korean new religions. When Korean new religions were called 'cheap' meanings such as pseudo religions, Korean religions, the thought of unifying all religion into one was mistreated as combining thoughts or jjamppong (mixing) religions. They were distortedly expressed that their doctrine had a complete system as religions, combined 3 religions moderately. The expression, 'the thought of unifying all religions into one' was used recently. Korean new religions have one thought ultimately. The Donghak thought, the Jeongyeok thought, and the Jeungsan thought are their own line. The thoughts of 3 religions in them are only their accessorial thoughts. So, the thought of unifying all religion into one is interpreted that Korean new religion ultimately claimed to succeed and complete the Fairy Tao in order to open a new era, absorbed three religions. In the doctrines of Korean new religions, there are the thoughts of Christianity Islam, the thought of nothing, Jeonggamrok, Gyeokamyourok, Poongsu secret, Yeok(易)thought, western New Age and the thought of muti-god of India including 3 religions.

4) The Theory of Building the Paradise, the Idea World

Examining Korean religious phenomenon and status, there are a lot of religions. More than 53% of people think of themselves as religious per the National Statistical Office. That is, more than majority of Koreans spend money and time in religions to satisfy their religious desires. Especially the number of Christians is decreasing; the number of Korean new religions is increasing. The factors that the number of Korean new religions increases are several. Among them, Korean new religions offer a reasonable and closer religious base to the culture and emotion of modern people than existing religion's doctrines. However, above all, an important factor is that Korean new religions suggest a hope of the paradise reasonably and strongly, a dream to overcome ignorance and sin and live happily forever that 3 religions cannot do. I found in my research that those conditions brighten the future of Korean new religions, gain persuasive of religionists. The afterlife view to go heaven after death lost persuasive decades ago to highly have developed modern civilization and spiritually developed Koreans. If religion does not suggest concrete ways to achieve physical immortality and go to the Idea world, the role and function of the religion is finished according to comparative religionists of Korea. Therefore, one among Korean new religious movement's features is building the Idea world, which is its creation's aim and its final aim. As this world is full of contradiction, irrationality, pain and sin, suggesting a new value and order and building an immortal world of posterior are the creators' intention. And the oriental Idea world is expressed as the Big One World, what describes it concretely and realistically is the Idea world in Korean new religion. Donghak Cheondo religion expresses the Idea world the paradise, which contains that everybody lives forever, not this decaying physical body or spirit lives forever, but changed into neohumans' spirit and body are both reborn as the Holy Spirit, and become immortal, at that time all things recover the immortal paradise. For example, Gang Jeung San expressed the Idea World as a fairyland. As his heavenly work and great open focused on the fairyland, it is very concrete. First material's abundance is accomplished, "people cook rice without lighting a fire, they do farming without getting mud on their hands. Trains go with a lot of things ten thousand miles in a short time." Gang Jeung San predicted the future of 100 years like he experienced them. Also he foretold "all humanity become one family". Furthermore, he predicted due to the changing of material and spirit, all anguishes would perish, and good health and long life era and 'a great ethics era' would come. Through studying the blood of Koreans and the thoughts of the ancient philosophy that Korean new religions came out, and a lot of prophetic books, the prediction that the Messiah of the Bible will appear in Korea is common in the east and west. People will see through this thesis that due to the advent of the Victor that emits the hidden manna, the secrets of the prediction in all the scriptures are revealed, the building the paradise is really progressed. The proof is the advent of white group who are practicing the immortal philosophy and the afterlife view of Samsedeungmyeong that are the neohumans cultures, soon its end will be revealed.

3. The Korean New Religions' Nickname

Korean new religions do not have their official terms because not only the existing religions are very exclusive to them but also the concept of new religion was not clearly established.
There are about 10 to indicate Korean new religions. Here are their names.
1) Similar Religion
When Korea was occupied by Japanese, Moorayama jijun(村山智順) named it examining Korean new religions for 10 years. He thought that Korean new religions were not primitive but similar religion. As they became a prop to inspire their spirit, new religions were persecuted by Japanese.
2) Heretical religion: It means a group that pretends religions, but it commits crime.
3) Korean Homemade religion: It is expressed by Korean government, it lowers Korean traditional religions.
4) Pseudo religion
Most Christianity call Korean new religions like that, it means false.
5) Faction religion: It means sectarianized religions.
6) Immature level religion: It means a religion that does not have a complete system as a general religion.
7) Folk religion: It comes from the process when scholars studied Korean new religions; it means they contain the hope of people.
8) Newly-rising religions: It has the opposite meaning of existing religions.
9) Sae(new) religions: It means as newly-rising religions, they should be renewed, the writer(the chairman of Korean New

Religion Academy) named it.
10) New religion : Nowadays, academia call commonly it, also Japanese use it by the created time. So they name recently created religions new new religions. The Victory Altar is a new new religion created in 1981, which will complete the aims of Korean new religions by the advent of the Victor Savior predicted in all the Scriptures. NRMs of Korea is a little different from those of other countries. I could find they represent the will of heaven and have their directions that awake the spirit of the the times. Then I will examine the role of NRMs of Korea that will influence the present and future.

4. The Role and Future of NRMs of Korea

First, I will examine the status of Korean new religions and discuss the role and future of Korean new religions. Korean new religions were distortedly mistreated as religious cults. Recently they are called the religion of a people, newly- risen religions, and new religions. As times changed, their awareness is changed. When all religions come first, to be welcomed is rare. At the beginning, they are considered to be cults, rigging cases, creators die the death or their religious body collapse. After overcoming the difficulties and blooming the truth, true religions are admitted as true religions, grow as the world religion. Now Korean new religions are in a transition period, they get out of being called pseudo, can reveal their original meaning as new religions. Until they come here, there are endeavors and sacrifice of all new religions as well as one religionist's tenacity and devotion. Like this, the role of Korean new religions is to prepare in order to save ignorant and sinful humanity and lead to the paradise. Now their role is not to dwell on their incomplete teaching but to adjust the law and culture of a new world, which is the condition to be saved. As they have missions to lead all humanity to the way of salvation, they look forward to the advent and their roles of a lot of neohumans to lead all humanity.

The last step of the theory of the Savior in Korean new religious movements

The Savior saves humanity from crisis and chaos. The creators of existing religions or Koreans new religions are saviors, too. So Tae San, the creator of one Buddhism, said, "At the end of times, people will suffer terrible things, and the Savior will appear with a law to lead all humanity and correct the heart of all humanity by turning the vigor of heaven and earth." Jeongsan who succeeded So Tae San told, "when posterior is open, the Savior will appear and change the world". There are two theories of the savior in new religions. One is that the creators of religion insist that they are saviors and the other is that future generations make them saviors. Su Woon, the creator of Donghak, did not say his status, but each religious sect served him as the Savior to save humanity. But Gang Jeung San revealed himself that he was the Savior. But there was no thesis about the Savior who will accomplish the last aim of Korean new religion. Uniquely, I revealed the Savior through studying the prophetic culture of Gyeoamyourok in Mejiro graduate school in Japan. I discussed the flow of NRMs of Korea and the ultimate aim in the thesis. Another thesis is that I explained how the Idea World will be built in volume 24 of Korean New Religious Academy Journal; it is sold and cited as scholars' research material through the Internet.

The ultimate aim of NRMs of Korea is to build the paradise and Korean new religions are preparing for a new age, but they do not tell the way concretely and realistically. Only the Victory

Altar suggests the definite way concretely and realistically and is building heaven by the hero of heaven. That is the reason that existing religions and Korean new religions with more than 50 years history are jealous of the Victory Altar, finally a senior president of Christianity forced the Savior to prison for 7 years by inciting new Christianity and big new religions.

The Direction and Future of Korean NRMs of Korea that Korean New religionists predict

The Korean religious history which started with the ancient God leading religion (fairy Tao) has been connected the era of multi-religions in contemporary by the three religions(Confucianism, Buddhism, the Chinese Taoism) inflowing in the era of the three States, unified Silla, Goryeo dynasty, and Chosen dynasty. They are Korean new religions that opened the era of multi- religions. As Donghak is the center of Korean new religions, since the ancient God leading religion(神教), thousands years later, Korea's indigenous faith appeared again. The history of Korean new religions is 150 years, but their doctrines have all contents as general religions. Furthermore, they try to stand in the center in overcoming the limit and contradictions of existing religions and to create a new era. That is the great open. So the thought of Korean new religions is that of the great open (the big change). The paradise is the world established by the great open. The paradise that the creators of new religions predicted means a physically contemporary science civilization. I think that the science civilization will not go further than the electronic era. The problem is the spiritual world. Material civilization is changed, but their spirit is not. New religions put commonly the change of spirit in that of great ethics and spirit. So when the great ethics civilization and science civilization harmonize, when humanity is respected, the welfare era of neo-humans will be realized. The necessities in changing humanity's spirit and building the paradise are the advent of the Victor and neohumans who are transcendent of birth, old age, sickness, and death. The Victory Altar has the theory of salvation and the Victor of the Bible, so a lot of Korean new religionists crowd there beyond their religions and are trained to become neohumans. That is a hope to humanity who wanders in a sinful and ignorant world. Therefore, the future of the Victory Altar and Korean new religions are bright.

CHAPTER II
The New View of Afterlife & the Secret of New Heaven

Where do all humans of the world of the 21th century have to go? How do they go to heaven? Where is the new heaven in Holy Scriptures? Will the collapse of all humans and the doomsday of the earth surely come? Now is the time for us to rethink about the new heaven and afterlife. In this crisis of material civilization, the aims of my thesis are as follows. First, I will suggest the right way that humans should go newly, a method that all humans become one and build a peaceful paradise. By revealing the hidden secret of God in the Bible, the Buddhist scriptures, and prophetic books, this thesis will be a compass to find out the way of going heaven to poor people who are wandering in darkness. Second, I will say through the predictions of God how humanity has to change such as the way of humans' life, values, and thinking that they have had until now to overcome the present situations. Finally, by revealing the philosophy of the new heaven and the predictions in the Holy Scriptures, I will surely show the people of the world that the wrong view of the afterlife has a very bad influence upon modern material civilization and moral culture. Also, I felt the necessity that I should reveal the true meaning of the heaven and whereabouts of the new heaven in the Holy Scriptures by reconsidering the definition and true meaning of the heaven, and the essence of the heaven in the Holy Scriptures. This paper is composed of the view of Korean existing new religions' afterlife and the new view of afterlife of Korean new religions that emerges as a new paradigm and pioneer of new spiritual movement. And this stream is connected by the root of the Korean ancient philosophy and Korean traditional religions. Korean new new religions are based on the thought of Hananim (God) which regards that humans are God. Their main thoughts are the Geabyeok (the Big change) thought, the immortal philosophy, and the supernatural being thought. I studied the experience of the followers who announce a new spiritual movement, the view of the future and the new heaven of Koreans new religions, the view of the afterlife of neo-humans, who dwell in the new heaven, the New Paradise that happens in their heart. In this thesis, I came to know that the components of heaven are the Sweet Dew; the hidden manna and the fruit of life in the Bible, and the advent of the Messiah, Jeongdoryeong. I found through the ancient thought of Koreans that the Koreans have waited for the Victor Jeongdoryeong, the Messiah. Therefore the thought is called by some researchers, the thought of Jeongdoryeong or Mireuk (Maitreya Buddha), the same meaning to the Messiah on the Bible. Further, while I studied the new Korean religions, I found that the philosophy of Hanmom(one body)of neo-humans will be the new best study that saves people and makes all religions and philosophies one. Therefore, in this respect, the thesis has a big meaning; I expect that by knowing the essence of Korean new religions, people will be able to surely find out the new heaven and the door of salvation in the future coming soon. Especially, I want to say that in my thesis, there are three important terms such as '新天(New Heaven)', '新地(New Earth)', '新人類(Neo-human)', which are necessary and have been hidden for completing heaven. The completion of the new heaven is accomplished by the work of the Holy Dew Spirit following the three processes, which are 'the advent of the Victor', 'Gaebyeok(the big change) of humans' mind', and 'the building of the paradise by neo-humans'. Besides through the predictions of the Bible, Korean prophecies, Chinese prophecies, and several scriptures, I studied the essence of new heaven and mysterious spiritual heaven which is accomplished in the bodies and mind of neo-humans.

1. New Values & the New View of Being and Death of the Victory Altar

The view of afterlife and the view of the exodus of the cycle of birth and death of the Victory Altar are that my present life is the afterlife of my ancestors; my ancestors' lives are my previous life. Therefore, if I get out of birth, aging, diseases, and death, I cut the causation of the three lives and enjoy nirvana. Therefore, thinking of this view, it is completely different from the view of afterlife of existing religions that people go to heaven after death. However, the will and endeavor to get out of the cycle of birth and death, to enjoy nirvana, to recover the nature of not dying Buddha (God) are a new view of the exodus of birth and death in new era. That is, it is another view of getting out of birth and death not to be conscious of death, not to adapt death, and try to overcome death. I have studied the immortal philosophy that is the view of the exodus of the cycle of birth and death to find out the whereabouts of dead spirit and the way of the exodus of birth and death.

Next, I will examine the new values of the exodus of birth and death of the Victory Altar. Through the phrase of the Bible "Humans like tombs!", we may think how we get out of the marsh of birth and death. The phrase makes people think of their aim philosophically. Where do humans come from and where do they go?" A lot of people study to solve this problem through all their lives. Although some scholars spent their lives solving this problem, nobody suggested the answer. Neither existing religions and new religions nor philosophy gave the answer.

1) The Values and Aim of Lives of the Victory Altar

My life is only once, how can I make my short life the most valuable? Everybody experiences the period of puberty that makes adolescence think of their identity and their philosophy of life. We have faced a lot of values since we were born. There are a lot of ways, split values, seeking, and objects of life before us. The young man's dream of becoming a president or a general is shrunk rapidly by realizing reality as they become old. Therefore, some people's aims are eating three meals a day, some people are studying, some do business, some become politicians, some participate in religious activities. Some spend their lives studying a maggot, others spend their lives studying in their laboratories, some spend their lives going and out prisons due to trying to steal big money. Therefore, when they distinguish themselves in some areas, they are old and come around the corner of death. People can enjoy their lives with healthy bodies. No matter how influential geniuses are, if they die, their bodies rot and disappear, and people cannot approach with their spirit. What is the use of their life?

Therefore, the values of life do not exist to dead people. In the end, the values of their lives were empty. They lived to die. As they did not have clear values, their values of life are finished meaninglessly. Life is lined once no matter how happy or sad people are. To dead people, their lives are ones to die. To people who have an aim to live forever, they live happily their whole lives for eternal life. Therefore, if people must live their lives, living with the hope of eternal life is not only the ground breaking mind of the Victory Altar's followers but also a meaningful philosophy of life. Only people who have the aim of eternal lives can feel a hope of life and feel value of life. I think the value of a person has determined their life-span and happiness. The members of the Victory Altar have their values in realizing of eternal life with living bodies, also being reborn as the Holy Spirit, returning God, and living as immortal being is their supreme values and happiness of life.

2) The View of Birth and Death of the Victory Altar

In the Victory Altar, the aim of faith is getting out of the circle of birth and death, returning to the original God, and enjoying eternal life. Therefore, they neither even think of the term of death nor use it. Therefore, those who say that my headache is so serious, that I could just die, I am so happy, that I could just die, I am so tired ,that I could just die, go to hell do not realize the sayings of the Seventh Angel. People are taken to tombs without being conscious because they are caught by Satan their controlling spirit, are deceived. They hurt themselves, and walk toward death. The members of the Victory Altar never use or think about the terms related to death. Also they try not to have a mind to die and keep the Law of Liberty. People in the area of alternative medicine and spirit science say if people talk about something, their bodies and minds recognize their saying and their bodies and mind are accomplished as their saying with help from their spiritual power. This fact is the result of the study of the science of spirit, which is higher than advanced science. The Victory Altar says that people die because of the wage of death on the basis of the Bible, James 1:15" Evil desire conceives and gives birth to sin; and sin, when it is full-grown, give birth to death." Romans 6:23", For sin pay its wage; death" 2 King14:6, "a person is put to be to death only for a crime he himself has committed". Because Self-Consciousness that is the root of desires controls people, they dies. That is the reality of death. The Victory Altar does not use the insane saying that people go to heaven after death. Also they are not deluded by such an illogical saying. Then what happens to dead people? According to the most universal common sense, people lose their consciousness when they die. Although there is much to be desired in proving whether the spirit leaves the body or not after death, the Bible says that after death, the spirit disappears. Also the Victory Altar's followers believe people die when a person's energy and spirit is destroyed completely. Therefore, there is nothing to be left after death. There is no difference in weight just before death and just after death; the body get cold gradually right after death. As soon as one dies, his/her blood stops, the temperature of the body becomes cold, it stiffens, finally blood and body rot, and becomes soil. There is nothing left any more. Only if he/she exists somewhere, he/she exists painfully in his/her children who are produced by his/ her blood, he /she faces his /her afterlife in his/her children's present world. Therefore, if people die, their lives' have no meaning and happiness and spirit finish, and nothing left. They should try desperately to be born as the Holy Spirit and to recover original their light by rooting out the factors to kill people. This is a different point from other new religions.

2. The Secret of New Heaven & the Advent of Heaven's Man

1) The View of New Heaven and Existing Heaven

Christianity still celebrates Easter, a physical revival. However, now is the time to suggest a new interpretation of heaven on the basis of the Bible. It is an important topic to humans who welcome new millennium; it will give a clue to solve the conflict and argument between religions. According to the Gallop polls, 85 % of American people who live in a society with advanced science believe heaven. Most humans are vaguely sure that their lives do not finish in the tomb. It is time to reveal the true meaning of heaven in order for all humans to become one. If people do not change the corrupt society, will dream to go to heaven after death come true? So far, humans have done an empty dream for the paradise that heaven is the prize at the final moment of their life without knowing the whereabouts of sin and the cause of death. In fact, the fixed thought of going to heaven after death becomes a hotbed of conflict between culture, religion, and status in the history of Christianity. They misunderstood heaven as another world, thought that they go to heaven by blindly believing in someone. Imagining that heaven is different from the present world, people expect to receive the comfort from the painful world, the result is just death. Like that, the history of Christianity has passed 2000 years, it is the time to rethink of after death going to heaven.

2)The New Definition and meaning of New Heaven, the paradise

(1) The Definition of Heaven

Luke17:21, 1Corintians3:16, and a hymn of Christianity starting with 'my spirit wear the grace of God' write that nor will people say, here it is or there it is, because the kingdom of God is within you, where God dwells, whether a thatched cottage or a palace, is heaven. The definition of heaven is where the Trinity dwells, God is the hero of heaven, and heaven is in humans' mind because God dwells there. Then in what kind of mind can heaven be accomplished? The man who completes God in His body by changing His mind can become the hero of the paradise. Here is an important prediction you should know. Why did New Heaven not exist so far? In what condition was God so far?

In the part of Dobusinin of 「Gyeokamyourok」, a Korean prophetic book with 100 percent's accuracy, says as follows. The predictions: God in the beginning waged a war against Satan, He lost to Satan, was deprived of the authority of ruling the universe, was locked in the prison of Satan and degenerated into all things and people. To reinstate the lost paradise, God had prepared for thousands years. The prediction says because the true paradise was not so far, people died by the spirit of death. Due to the advent of the Victor who will end the sinful world, a new era has begun according to the hidden secret of heaven in all scriptures such as the Bible, the Buddhist books, prophetic books of Korea and China.

(2) The place where the paradise will be built and the whereabouts of the gate of heaven

As I already said above, heaven is built in the mind of humans, heaven is where God dwells. In fact, the words of God and the whereabouts of heaven were deeply hidden, so normal people cannot understand prophetic books, and some leaders of religion interpret heaven of the Bible differently. John Blanchard, the founder of Planet Rock Youth Ministries, said, "I do not believe that people fly with wings to the heaven after death like Cupid. Heaven is the place where we should go with our physical body and religion should suggest people how to live". In fact, because heaven is built in the mind of humans, they should not waste time vaguely thinking that heaven will be built in other world. The Bible tells that God Himself is the life of humans, so God exists in blood as life. However, there are few people who know this fact. Now, God of the Holy Spirit that overcomes the authority of death can become the hero of heaven, the man who accompanies the God becomes the gate of heaven and can build the true paradise according to the Bible. To go to this heaven and experience Him, they should know the essence of God.

(3) The Essence of God

What is the essence of God?

In Genesis 9:4 and John 1:1~3 in the Bible, they say about what the essence of God is. According to John1:1~3, "in the beginning was the Word, and the Word was with God, and the Word was God." Also, according to Numbers 16:22, 27:16, God is the life of all flesh, life is in the heart, According to Proverbs 4:23, the life of a creature is in the blood according to Leviticus 17:11, the blood is the life. Taken these words together, the essence of God is life, life is just blood, blood is the life of the body including the spirit, the spirit is mind, the mind is the house of God. Therefore, God existing in the blood of humans is the light of humans, the source of life, and the light of the Holy Spirit, The owner of heaven who can give salvation to all people should overcome death and be reborn as the Holy Spirit. Such the Victor God is called New Heaven or heaven. The Bible says that the Victor Savior God reveals the secret of new heaven to people, those who are tainted with sins cannot see God. However, Neo-humans, the children of light can see God. This interpretation is very Biblical.

All living things emit the light of life. Modern physicists have already said that atoms compose all materials, neutrons are in the nucleus of atoms, and electrons go around neutrons. The power of making electrons go around neutrons is not automatic.

The power of life makes them turn around. Having the power of life is being alive, and being alive means having life. On the other hand, dying is losing life.

If the essence of life is God, the essence of death is Satan, the soul of devil. Then what is life? Life is just God. Satan, the spirit of devil, has no life; it has only the spirit of death. The spirit of death rides God, life, and finally kills God. Therefore, humans dying mean that God that is the root of life dies and the light energy of God perishes at the moment. All living things and the universe were originally immortal God (Buddha) who was the light of the Trinity. At that moment the two Gods among the Trinity were occupied by the spirit of death, Satan, and Satan had deprived its light energythree God, separated them into female and male, and they have died until now.

(4) The Symbol of New Heaven

The hero of New Heaven is the Victor God, what is His symbol? Like doctors should have a qualification, the Victor God has His symbol according to the Bible, the Buddhist books, and prophetic books. Like I said above, New Heaven is the Victor God, what happens when the Victor appears? I will introduce the result of my study through participant observation and studying scriptures.In Korea, the revolution of religion is happening, some phenomenon that announcesthe advent of New Heaven. For example, the secret that the presidential candidate who New Heaven chooses become a president, the source of economic development, the changing reformation of religion, wrong predictions of weather forecasts, the secret of typhoons avoiding the Korean Peninsula, the secret of continuing abundant harvests of Koreans, the dry rainy seasons, a pillar of cloud and the Sweet Dew falling from the sky on a fine day, the changed minds of the followers of the Victory Altar are all phenomenon out of all knowledge. Especially, the Holy Dew Spirit, the symbol of New Heaven, is making humane minds heaven. I presented a paper in detail about the Holy Dew Spirit in the seminar of new religion in Taiwan in 2011. Among the three factors of composing heaven, the Sweet Dew which is the most important factor. I will introduce the three factor of composing heaven next.

(5) The Symbol of the Victor in the world scriptures
The Hidden Manna and the Secret of the Holy Dew Spirit

Hosea 14:5 and Joel 2:28~30 foretold, "God descends as the light of the Holy Dew Spirit." The Israel people lived on manna for forty years according to the Book of Exodus16:13 and Number11: 6-9. If the manna of Moses period is a physical manna, the Hidden manna in the Bible, the Holy Dew Spirit of the true Messiah, is a spiritual manna. The Holy Dew Spirit in the Bible is the hidden manna of New Heaven that makes dying all creatures be reborn as the Holy Spirit and live forever in happiness. Revelation 2:17 "He who has an ear, let him hear what the Spirit says to the churches. To him who overcomes, I will give some of the hidden manna." These words mean that the man who has the hidden manna is the Victor. The Dew is an immortal manna. "Your dew is like the dew of the morning; the earth will give birth to her dead" according to Isaiah 26:19.

Dew did not fall after Moses' times. Much later, Isaiah, a great prophet, predicted as follow, "But your dead will live; their bodies will rise. You, who dwell in the grave, wake up and shout. Your dew is like the dew of the morning; the dew will give birth to her dead" in Isaiah 26:19. This predicted, "if the Savior who pours down the Dew appears, death would perish." The Dew is not a physical food, but a spiritual food. It means just an immortal manna. Also John 6:27 says, "Do not work for food that spoils, but for food that endures to eternal, which the Son of Man will give you. On him God the Father has placed his seal of approval." 1Corinthians 15:54 writes, "When the perishable has been clothed with the imperishable and the mortal with immortality, then the saying that is written will come true: "Death has been swallowed up in victory." Therefore, the words "humans' life span is like trees" are accomplished after the Holy Dew Spirit appears.

The Sweet Dew in Buddhist scriptures

Sakyamuni predicted 'the Dharma of the Sweet Dew' in Buddhist scriptures. Let's see how Buddhist scriptures foretell about the Reincarnate Maitreya Buddha.

The Buddhist Scriptures express the Sweet Dew(甘露)as the light of great nirvana that the Reincarnated Maitreya Buddha pours out The whole Buddhist scriptures such as Great Nirvana Sutra, Dharma Flower Sutra, and Flower Adornment Sutra say that the Sweet Dew is the symbol of the Reincarnated Maitreya Buddha.

The other self of the Reincarnate Maitreya Buddha comes from TV screen during a sermon.

According to volume 26 of Flower Adornment Sutra, the Reincarnated Maitreya Buddha, who can fill the universe with His other selves for an instance, pours down the Sweet Dew and removes the agonies of people. According to Sasangpum(四相品) part of the Great Nirvana Sutra volume 5 says, "There are no death here because of the Sweet Dew(是處無死), the man who pours out this Sweet Dew is the man who reaches nirvana." According to the part of life span of the Great Nirvana volume 2, Sakyamuni said only when the Dharma of the Sweet Dew comes, people would reach nirvana. Also, the part of 4-2 the nature of the Reincarnate Maitreya Buddha of the Great Nirvana Sutra the volume 5 tells about the essence and the origin of the word of the Sweet Dew concretely as follows: The Buddha is the existence that neither delivers children, nor dies, nor collapses, nor catches diseases. It means nirvana; death is not here because of the Sweet Dew. This Sweet Dew is nirvana. In other words, it is the body of Dharma. When a man dies, his body collapses and his life perishes. Like this the Scriptures said, the basic aim of the Dharma of the Buddhism is to get out of the circle of being born, catching diseases, and dying, and to live forever enjoying bliss. Also, Bupgugyeong Annyeong part (法句經 安寧品) predicted if you get out of the circle of birth and death, you should receive the Sweet Dew.

The authority and symbol was given to the Victor

Now, I will examine the prediction about the fruit of life in the world scriptures. The predictions about the fruit of life on the basis of the Bible. According to Revelation 2:26-28 in the Bible, "I will give the morning star to him who overcomes and does my will to the end; I will give authority over the nations. 'He will rule them with an iron scepter; he will dash them to pieces like pottery." According to Revelation 2:7, "He will give the right to eat from the tree of life to him who overcomes." In Revelation 2:17, it says, "God will give some of the hidden manna and a white stone with a new name written on it, known only to him who receives it. Revelation 3:12 says, "Him who overcomes, I will make a pillar in the temple of my God. Never again will he leave it. I will write on Him the name of my God, and the name of city of my God, the new Jerusalem, which is coming down out of heaven from my God; I will also write on Him my new name." Also Revelation 2:11 says, "He who overcomes will not be hurt at all by the second death." Revelation 3:21, "To him who overcomes, I will give the right to sit with on my throne, just as I sat down on God throne." It means God occupies the body of the Victor and becomes one with the Victor. That is, God is the Victor, the Victor is God. Like this, Revelation which is the last part of the Bible volume 66 says almost about the Victor, because if the Victor appears, immortality that is the aim of the Bible is expected to be accomplished. Therefore, God in John shouted the Victor to appear. Here what we should know is that the Victor, the Savior, and Israel indicate one person. As God is the Alpha and the Omega, God of the beginning was reborn as God of consummation became the Victor Savior and came to this world. The Savior is the man who was reborn as the Holy Spirit in Korea, the land in the Far East corner like the prediction of Isaiah 41 1: 9.

3. New Doctrine of the Victory Altar by the Tongsijeok Samse Deungmyeong (通時的三世燈明)

According to the Seventh Angel in the Victory Altar, all humans should awake from long sleep facing Samse Deungmyeong (三世燈明)'s era when the salvation of the previous life, this life, and the afterlife is accomplished in this life at one time, they should be reborn as the Holy Spirit, the condition of original God. What is the previous life? People say they can see the previous life through contacting another spirit in them by using special method. In fact, that is not the previous life; it is only contacting some awaking spirit among a lot of spirit which is embedded in subconscious. If it is wrongly changed, the changed spirit become the owner of the body and becomes crazy. Centering me now, the lives of the ancestors are my previous life(前世), my present life(現世) is my ancestor's afterlife, my afterlife(來世) is connected to my children, strictly speaking, all genetic information and traits are connected to this world through blood and lineage, therefore, only this world exists. Looking at these three lives with Tonsijeok(通時的=transcending time) view and explaining it with the principle of Samse Deungmyeong(三世燈明) were possible through the Seventh Angel's the principle of blood, the core theory of the philosophy of immortality. Therefore, by attaining the nature of Buddha with living bodies, that is, by being reborn as the Holy Spirit, not only all ancestors but also I can achieve salvation and three lives' dream (前世, 現世, 來世) come true in me. That is the view of the exodus of birth and death of the Victory Altar. People believe vaguely that the previous life, this world, and afterlife are separated. That is a quietly superficial thought. Like I said above, all lives and traits of people's ancestors are passed down to their offspring through blood, compose their offspring's bodies and mind in this world, and becomes the substance that moves their offspring's spirit. That is, people's afterlife(來世) exists in blood of their offspring. Therefore, my ancestors' nature and experiences have a close relationship with my style of behaviors and mind's working and influences a lot my life in the blood. If ancestors had a talent in music, among the descendants, there is surely a person who inherits the genetic material. If there were violent behaviors in some family, their violent character is revealed in their children according to genetics. Because all information has been recorded, saved, and has been passed down today. Therefore, all humans' original sins of 6000 years, a hereditary sin, and people committing sins in this world are here in their descendants 'bodies and are reflected in this world. And my afterlife is decided by my conditions of this world. Also, my previous life is the lives that my ancestors lived, the ancestors are living as my existence, as blood in this world, as all the sins and karma are connected and are passed down to me, the blood of my ancestors exists as my life and mind in this world (現世)of mine. Therefore, the previous life, this life and afterlife coexist in the blood at this moment. If I have a good mind, which washes the karma of the previous life, establishes heaven in ancestors' afterlife, and that is doing my best in this world. On the contrary, if I have an evil mind, that adds karma to the previous life, establish hell in my afterlife, and means I do not live a good life. Therefore, those who live for eternal life have the eternal present and also present time when they move is important for them. Those who live for eternal life forget feeling left from the previous life and illusion of afterlife and think of the present for eternal life. Additionally, they think of only Neo-humans who are reborn as the Holy Spirit and possess eternal life. Like that, those who are reborn as the Holy Spirit have no agonies about birth and death. And then, the Buddhist Sutra say that a Neo-human has neither birth nor death, that is, neither are they born nor die. They have only eternal life of a new level, the heaven of the present, in forever happiness. Perfect God is never conscious of time and space. Living shackled to the past and living in illusion of the future eat the lives of people. The mind that does not look back the past and does not expect the future is the life of God, which is the mind of true humans, God, or Buddha according to the theory of the Victory Altar. When the view of afterlife that people go to heaven after death is revealed as fallacy, all existing religions that were on the basis of the view of afterlife will be destroyed someday. Also, for thousands years, religions have been formed on the basis of the view of afterlife escaping reality, even they have not known the essence of God, they have pretended they are holy groups and have deceived people, but soon their scams will be revealed at one time. Thinking of this result, those who are awaken spiritually will guess it will be revolutionary accidents the proclaiming of the view of the exodus of the cycle of birth and death. Thinking from the philosophical aspect of immortality and the view of afterlife of the principle of blood of the Victory Altar, the view of afterlife that people go to heaven after death is a great illusion. The Seventh Angel already concluded that the view of going to heaven after death is not accepted in the modern society when genetic engineering and the science of life are advanced highly. Judging by the most universal experiences, unless people are reborn as the Holy Spirit, and attain neutral nature by achieving nirvana, they die and their spirit is destroyed. Therefore, the thought that spirit leaves the body after death is an anachronism and there is no method to prove that spirit leaves the body after death. There is no difference in weight just before death and just after death. Like this, Camper who studies about after death as a medical scientist of Germany supports the Seventh Angel's theory, and he revealed his study as follows "When humans die, they perish as material, nothing is left. I observed 8000 patients nearly to death with a special device that can record 1 /one million minute's wave." He tried to find whether the spirit leaves the body right before death or right after death, there is nothing leaving except gas from the body." I think the view of going to heaven after death does not make sense. Right after death, the body starts to be cold, the circulation of blood stops, the body stiffens, finally the blood decays, flesh decays, even the bones decays, and becomes soil. One lump of clay of vain spirit remains like you that did not transcend birth and death during your life, your children that are another lump of agony and sins that will die in pain will leave after your death. Nothing is left except those. There is neither heaven nor hell that exists separated from human life. Heaven and hell exist only in humans' mind. If I am happy at this moment, the moment you are in heaven, if I am unhappy at his moment, the moment you are in hell. This view is that of birth and death of the Victory Altar and they look dispassionately at the realities and try to get out birth, aging, diseases, and death through practicing asceticism. Therefore, I think their new transcending view of the exodus of birth and death is quietly rational.

CHAPTER III
The Ultimate Aim of NRMs in Korea & "The Law of Liberty" of the New Era

The aim of my thesis is to send the message that humanity will have the era of light by new heaven (the Victor God) overcoming darkness. I will announce the hidden manna of a new heaven and the secret of salvation that were revealed by the Victor. Plus, the Idea World that so far countless prophets, philosophers, and religionists have waited come into view in our era. Second, considering the way of humanity's peace, examining the philosophy of salvation that makes all humanity one and save them through the neo-humanity's culture, I will introduce the result. Third, I will introduce the Law of Liberty that will be the basic to the society of new heaven and new earth ideologies, the Hanmoum Philosophy will be a new philosophy and new study in the new era. Furthermore, I will contemplate the culture of neo-humans that keep the rule of heaven; this will complete a new world, making an end station of the world new religions. The world new religions are on the road to pluralism, it need doctrines of respecting humanity, a harmonious win-win. Fourth, I will consider the cultural structure of the future of neo-humans who will appear in the New Religions Movement. Finally, I will examine the process of the advent of neo-humans, the view of the world of neo-humans, the secret of being reborn as neo-humans, and the image of the future of the paradise in the prophetic books and scriptures of each religion. Humanity's philosophy determines his living environment, his behavior, his personality, and his face's shape. In this respect, my paper is very important because it will offer the clues to solving problems of the aim of humanity's life, the essence of humanity, the theory of religion, the theory of God, and the true value of humanity.

1. The Ultimate Aim of Korean New Religions

First, to study Korean new religions and to know its ultimate aim, if one does not know the old thought of Koreans, he/she cannot know the phenomenon of Korean new religions and the stream of the world new religions. There has been a thought of transcendent men from the old times. The Tao has been passed down as Tao of the taste for arts (風流道) in Koreans, which changed the dark world from the ancient times. The history of the Korean people spans 5000 years. It has the thoughts of its foundation, which are to widely help and love humanity and to respect heaven. Those thoughts are a perfect ideology and the basic thoughts of all religions. Because they had the very outstanding thoughts, the thought of 'Innaecheon' was formed by Mr. Choi SuWoon in 1860. 'Innaecheon' means that humans are heaven(God). Furthermore, it was sublimated as a philosophy that the conscience of humanity is God. The key point of those thoughts is that the essence of humanity came from God, the existence of bright light. The thought is 'the thought of One Big Bright Light'. Also there was 'a thought of God' that humanity is heaven and God. Korean new religions are based on them and their aim is building the new heaven where humanity neither becomes old nor dies. Building the recovered paradise is the aim of the western religions as well as that of Korean new religion.

That is, the ultimate aims of Korean New Religion Movement are just to make a new heaven and to accomplish eternal life without death and agony. To build the paradise, the Victor (the Maitreya Buddha in Buddhism, Jeongdoryeong that is the Savior of Koreans) appeared. And the building of the paradise has started. Humanity has waited for the Savior Victor for thousands years. Pseudo prophets and a lot of shepherds deceived and confused people that they were the Saviors. However, the man who pours down the Hidden Manna is the Victor Savior according to the Bible, the Reincarnated Maitreya Buddha in Buddhist scriptures(the Amita Sutra, the Lotus Sutra, the Nirvana Sutra), and Jeongdoryeong(正道靈) in a Korean prophetic Book, 「Gyeokamyourok(格菴遺錄)」 with 100 percent accuracy.

The conception of eternal life in 「Gyeokamyourok」 contains the meaning of immortal life in a physical body. Also, this study focuses on the new movements of new religions through the philosophy of eternal life occurring in Korea. Why? They have the same dream to pursue eternal life in this world in being alive, not going to heaven after death or the land of happiness. Especially, according to the prophecies of 「Gyeokamyourok」, the GamRo-HaeIn(甘露海印) and Holy Dew Spirit is the key of not only the salvation of humanity and but also the establishing the new heaven in this world. Then I will examine what the new

---

1) Gyeoamyourok was written by Namsago 450 years ago, in Korea. It predicted definitely the day of Korean dynasty's collapse, the day of finishing of the Japanese colonial, the Korean War, Korean presidents' family name, and so on. It writes that the God in the beginning lost to Satan, which has the authority of death. So the world became a mortal one. That is the secret of the God in the beginning. God revealed His secret in Gyeokamyourok through Nam Sa Go, a Korean, 450 years ago. Gyeokamyourok tells about the cause and the result that the Garden of Eden became the Lost Paradise. Furthermore it records that Jeongdoryeong appears with the Holy Dew Spirit and builds an immortal world. It also predicts the way of overcoming the mysterious diseases in the end of the times.

heaven is, what the difference between the new heaven and the existing view of heaven. Also I will explain why God hid the secret of the new heaven through Gyeoamyourok.

1) The Meaning of the New Heaven and its Secret

The definition of heaven is where the Trinity dwells, God is the hero of heaven, heaven is in humans' mind because God dwells there. Then in what kind of mind can heaven be accomplished? The man who completes heaven in His body can become the hero of the paradise. Koreans have had the thought of Innaecheon since the old times. The thought has been connected with ritual performances. The thought of Innaecheon is to respect heaven and life. Also Koreans had a thought of hoping for the Messiah. Koreans waited for Jeongdoryeong who would build heaven. In conclusion, the ultimate aim of Korean new religions is to construct heaven where people do not die, but live happily forever without pain or agony.

2) The Meaning of the New Heaven in the view of 'Innaecheon' and the Thought of the Big Change

Examining 「Samilsingo」, 「Handangogi」, 「Chamejeongyeogyeong」, and so on, I found Koreans recorded thousands years ago that all humanity is the children of God, they came from heaven. I will introduce the recoding that Koreans believed the one and the only God and have waited for a new world.

Mr. Underwood, a missionary of Korea, gave the surprising fact that Koreans have served the one and only God of ancient time. Mr. Underwood said that Koreans have believed God as the one and only God. He decided to use God instead of Jehovah to do missionary work and succeeded. This philosophy of God has been connected to the thought of regarding humans being as God and has come to face the era of bearing fruit of the work of the Holy Spirit.

(1) What is the Thought of 'Innaecheon'?

The thought of 'Innaecheon' means that humanity is God. Performing rituals, the thought of respecting life became Korean traditional religions and a representative philosophy of Koreans. Searching the history of Korean new religions such as 'Cheondo religion', 'Jeungsan religion', One Buddhism, I could they had wishes to change the mortal world into an immortal one. That is a fetal of the thought of Innaecheon, which is a basic root to make a movement of Korean new religions.

(2) The Thought of the Big Change

What is the thought of the Big Change? Examining its meaning, it means opening something. That is, speaking easily, it indicates opening something new. The thought is a representative philosophy and Korean new religion that contains the will of heaven to change the sinful and mortal world into an immortal one. Tao of the taste for arts and the thought of transcendent men have been passed through oral tradition thousands years before the thought of the Maitreya Buddha and the Messiah came, they were shaped up as the movement of Big Change 100 years ago, appear a real movement for building heaven. Speaking of this in the term of the western new religion, it is a process to realize the building of heaven and the thought of hope for the Messiah, it is explained as a movement of new new religions or a new age movement. Next, I will tell you the three necessities to build heaven.

3) The Three Necessities to Build Heaven

The three factors are the victorious God(新天=New Heaven), the promised earth(新地=New Earth), and New Humans(Neo-humans=新人類). I came to know through studying Korean new religions and a prophetic book that the three things are necessary to build heaven. Gyeokamyourok writes that the man who has the three factors and revealed the secrets of heaven that were sealed in the Bible is admitted as Jeongdoryeong(the Victor Savior). That is, the victorious God should come first to the world, another thing is that the promised earth should be secured, that is, the building of heaven is possible when the promised earth(新地=New Earth)where heaven will be built is secured. Revelation of the Bible writes 'the promised earth' as 'the white stone. The other thing is neohumans that will live in the new heaven and the new earth. Unless the people of heaven(新人類=New Humans(Neo-humans)) who are reborn as the nature of God appear, the heaven can never be completed. I want to name the three conditions to build heaven the three necessary factors. These new heaven(the Victorious God), a new earth, and neohumans are keys to change the world, they are the result of the God preparing for 6000 years not by the power or efforts of humanity. Gyeokamyourok expressed that Jeongdoryeong looks like a human but he is God from heaven '似人不人 天神降'. The movement of Korean new religion heralds the reinstating of the Garden of Eden, its center is Sosa(素砂 meaning a white stone) area, Bucheon city in Korea according to Gyeoamyourok. The Savior can be admitted by fulfilling all of the predictions of the scriptures, by the phenomenon of his religion is the same as the predictions. I revealed through my master's thesis in Mejiro graduate school in Japan that the predictions about Jeongdoryeong in Gyeokamyourok correspond with the real movement and evidences of the Victor Savior, Mr. Cho Hee Sung in the Victory Altar. I wrote in my graduate thesis the meaning of heaven and its essence in Korean prophetic books, the key points of the movements of Korean new religions, and where their last station is. Next, I will say the changing procedure of heaven and earth to build the paradise.

4) Three Steps of the Big Change(開闢=GaeByeok)

The recording of 'the Big Change' was often written in the prophetic books, Korean new religions cite the term frequently in their scriptures. I could see through the scriptures of Korean new religions that Korean new religions preach citing the term while illustrating the last phenomenon of Korean new religions, the captain of the Big Change, and how people can find the captain and be reborn as the Holy Spirit. The Korean new religions tell the neutral era of the Garden of Eden as the prior heaven, the Lost paradise as the posterior era, and the era of changing the sinful world and opening a new one as the posterior Big Change. So the era before the Victor Savior appeared was named the posterior era. Koreans have waited for an immortal era and the advent of the Savior(Jeongdoryeong Gyeokamyourok, the Victor in the Bible, the Maitreya Buddha in Buddhism). Almost Korean new religions which are based on Korean traditional religion and the eastern philosophy insist that their religion's founder is the Savior. Who is the true Savior who will open the paradise? The work to reveal the starting point and the final of building heaven is the duty of the scholars of not only Korean new religions but also the world new religions.

Now I will explain the process of the Big Change simply. To understand the history of the Big Change, if one does not possess the old thought, language, philosophy, the nature of Koreans, and a new paradigm of Korean new new religion, he/she cannot see the paradise, the work of salvation, and the secret of heaven. Unless one understands the thought of Innaecheon, the thought of the Big Change, the thought of transcendant men, and the thought of Jeongdoryeong, it is very difficult to know the work of heaven, the direction and aim of Korean new religions. Let's see the process of the Big Change. I will explain the three process of the Big Change macroscopically and microscopically.

(1) The Process in the Aspect of the Universe(人心靈界→地上物界 →天上法界)

The material civilization of the earth and the principle of nature will be changed by neohumans who achieve their inner change. And then the principle of the universe will be changed into that of brilliant light.

　①The change of humanity's inner or spirit
　②The global change through the change of killing culture or society
　③The beginning of the universal change

(2) The Process of the Big Change from the Aspect of the Small Universe(天→人→地)
　①A changed new heaven by the advent of victorious God
　②The advent of neohumans by the inner change of humanity(the spiritual change)
　③ An immortal new earth by the completion of an immortal heaven. Considering in the macroscopic aspect and in the microscopic aspect, I explained the process of the Big Change in two ways.

Like I mentioned above, in order for heaven to be built, the change of the New Heaven, the New Earth, and Neo-humans(三才開闢) should be first fulfilled.

Next, I think that in the procedure of heaven and earth to be changed, the Big Change will be progressed through three steps. Speaking of it easily, the changing of decaying and dying heaven and earth is achieved gradually. To save humanity who was tainted with thousands of years of sins and the custom of Satan, a short and sudden change causes a lot of victims. So I think the change goes along in the order of a new heaven, neohuamans, and a new earth. Here we need to know who has the key of heaven, who the subject and object of the Big Change are. Because the men who do not have the key of heaven confuse people by insisting as the Savior, new religions need to recheck the hero of the Big Change, what his symbols are. Then, checking two symbol and evidence among around 100 evidences of the Victor, people can see whether the Savior is true or pseudo one in the scriptures.

5) The Secret of the Manna (the key of new heaven), and the White Stone

Like I said above, only the man who has a key of the new heaven can open, complete the new heaven. Also, only the man who knows the secrets of the manna and the white stone precisely is qualified as the Victor according to the scriptures such as the Bible and the Buddhist books. So far the Victor of the Victory Altar has the two conditions of the Victor among the founders of Korean new religion. The Victor who leads the Victory Altar has not only the above two conditions but also more around 100 evidences of the Victor that the scriptures predicted already thousands years ago. So I came to study the Victor of the Victory

Altar intensely. The Victory Altar revealed the secrets of the hidden manna and the white stone in the Bible and the Buddhist books, sends a message of the Victor to the world. I wrote the result of my study in the journal of the Korean New Religion Academy volume 24. The Korean new religions are jealous at the Victory Altar because it can tell the philosophy of eternal life and the view of Samsedeungmyeong after life in a physical body that everybody wants. You refer the journal of the Korean New Religion Academy volume 24. Korean Christianity became tense by the advent of the Victor persecuted the Victory Altar and the Victor centering high-ranking government officials. They distorted the Victory Altar through mass media and even enforced the Victor to jail for 7 years. The new movement of Korean new new religions has occurred for decades, but the existing religions do not adjust to the view of after life in a physical body and stick to the view of going to heaven after death. By the point of the advent of the Victor and neohumans, the new religions which do not do their role as religion are declining and are disappearing gradually. Many Christians use their religion as their business not using them for their salvation. The religion which suggests the theory of salvation, the hidden manna, the secret of the white stone, and the secrets of heaven can exist as a winner according to the scriptures. The righteous man and neohumans will unify all the religions, philosophy, theology, and science of the world, become a leader of the new heaven, lead all humanity of the world to the new heaven according to a prophetic poem of Tagore of India.

Now I will reveal the secrets of the white stone and the hidden manna, show you the phenomenon of the Victory Altar which tells about the philosophy and the secret of immortality through some pictures I took pictures. I took many pictures of the Holy

Dew Spirit while I studied the Victory Altar.

The light goes in spiral not in straight line. You can see countless particles of life light. Mr. Gordon, an American expert for appraisal of pictures, told that the light of the Victor's nirvana

cannot be imitated by the technic of humanity. It is a spiritual material, the spirit of the Victor God. The Bible says, "God is light". That is, they are the pictures of God. If the light comes to your body, you will feel fresh and happy because it kills your ego. It goes to only pure and innocent people like children. God knows who is pure or sinful. Usually the light of God follows the followers of the Victory Altar day and night and keeps them. So they feel happy all the time because God is the spirit of happiness. I received spiritual eyes to see God from decades ago. So I can say about the work of new heaven and the last stop of Korean new religions in detail. Everybody can take pictures of God with their cameras in the Victory Altar. Some pure people can see God with their naked eyes. That is the difference between the other religions and the Victory Altar. Also if you open your mind, God comes to you because you are his sons. He wants to occupy your body to make you immortal God. Then God kills the spirit of death in your Body. So if you keep receiving the spirit of God, your body is changed into an immortal one. What is true religion and the definition of religion? Eliade and the Chicago Schools did not give the answer. Also what is the secret of heaven, where the last stop of the world new religions is, what philosophy and science can make all humanity into one? I will offer the answers to the questions of the world new religions through my thesis or international seminars. Further I will reveal the result of case study through the journal of the culture of neohumans continually until all humanity can see the advent of the Savior. The Holy Dew Spirit, the hidden manna, is the essence of God, it is the basic factor to form a new heaven. However, only a few scholars of Korean new religion know the fact. The researchers of Korean new religions are ignorant about the will of heaven, a new paradigm of the movement of Korean new religions, never studied the hidden manna (the Holy Dew Spirit). So my study will become a fresh shocking. I already finished my thesis of 20 years about the hidden manna. Where the Sweet Dew does not fall, there is no salvation, and the paradise cannot be completed according to the scriptures. The fact is a key point of all the scriptures. The religion which cannot reveal the essence of neohumans and the hidden manna are not suitable to the movement of new religions and get out of the right way. So I think they cannot give the hope of salvation to people and their value will disappear gradually. This is the result of my study of 20 years about Korean new religions. The Sweet Dew is a core factor that the world new religions should study. Here are the predictions about the Sweet Dew in the Bible and the Buddhist scriptures.

1) The Sweet Dew in the Buddhist Scriptures

Sakyamuni predicted 'the Dharma of the Sweet Dew' in the Buddhist scriptures. Let's see how the Buddhist scriptures foretell about the Reincarnate Maitreya Buddha. The Buddhist Scriptures express the Sweet Dew(甘露)as the light of great nirvana that the Reincarnated Maitreya Buddha pours out. The whole Buddhist scriptures such as the Great Nirvana Sutra, the Dharma Flower Sutra, and the Flower Adornment Sutra say that the Sweet Dew is the symbol of the Reincarnated Maitreya Buddha.

According to volume 26 of the Flower Adornment Sutra, the Reincarnated Maitreya Buddha, who can fill the universe with His other selves for an instance, pours down the Sweet Dew and removes the agonies of people. According to Sasangpum(四相品) part of the Great Nirvana Sutra volume 5, "There are no death here because of the Sweet Dew(是處無死), the man who pours out this Sweet Dew is the man who reaches nirvana."

According to the part of life span of the Great Nirvana volume 2, Sakyamuni said only when the Dhrama of the Sweet Dew comes, people would reach nirvana. Also, the part of 4-2 the nature of the Reincarnate Maitreya Buddha of the Great Nirvana Sutra the volume 5 tells about the essence and the origin of the word of the Sweet Dew concretely as follows: The Buddha is the existence that neither delivers children, nor dies, nor collapses, nor catches diseases. It means nirvana; death is not here because of the Sweet Dew. This Sweet Dew is nirvana. In other words, it is the body of Dharma. When a man dies, his body collapses and his life perishes. Like this the Scriptures said, the basic aim of the law of the Buddhism is to get out of the circle of being born, catching diseases, and dying, and to live forever enjoying bliss. Also, Bupgugyeong Annyeong part (法句經 安寧品) predicted if you get out of the circle of birth and death, you should receive the Sweet Dew.

2) The Manna in the Bible

Manna is a miracle food from heaven, according to Exodus 16:14-31, Numbers 11:6-9, Deuteronomy (8:3), Nehemiah 9:20-21 Psalm (78:23-24), John (6:31), Revelation (2:17) in the Bible. When Moses took the Israel people to the desert from Egypt, there was no food with them. So they almost starved to death. They complained to Moses. Therefore, he prayed to God. The Lord of God said, "You will eat meat fully in the evening, eat rice cake in the morning." In that evening, quails covered the camp place and the next morning, dew fell down densely on the ground, the dew disappeared and something white and round like frost piled fully there. Moses said to people "God gave us this food; take the amount of food you can eat." This food has covered their camp site. They called the food 'manna'. As it was rotten after one day, they should bring the amount they could eat for one day; they were permitted 4 liter for each person. The Israel people lived on manna for forty years according to the Book of Exodus16:13 and Number11: 6-9. If the manna of Moses period is a physical manna, the Hidden manna in the Bible, the Holy Dew Spirit of the true Messiah, is a spiritual manna. The Holy Dew Spirit in the Bible is the hidden manna of New Heaven that makes dying all creatures be reborn as the Holy Spirit and live forever in happiness. Revelation 2:17 "He who has an ear, let him hear what the Spirit says to the churches. To him who overcomes, I will give some of the hidden manna." These words mean that the man who has the hidden manna is the Victor. The Dew is an immortal manna. Dew did not fall after Moses' times. Much later, Isaiah, a great prophet, predicted as follow, "But your dead will live; their bodies will rise. You, who dwell in the grave, wake up and shout. Your dew is like the dew of the morning; the dew will give birth to her dead "in Isaiah 26:19. This predicted, "if the Savior who pours down the Dew appears, death would perish." The Dew is not a physical food, but a spiritual food. It means just an immortal manna. Also John 6:27 says, "Do not work for food that spoils, but for food that endures to eternal, which the Son of Man will give you. On him God the Father has placed his seal of approval." 1Corinthians 15:54 writes, "When the perishable has been clothed with the imperishable and the mortal with immortality, then the saying that is written will come true: "Death has been swallowed up in victory." Therefore, the words "humans' life span is like trees" are accomplished after the Holy Dew Spirit appears. Then, let me tell you where a new heaven will be built, the law of neohumans predicted in the scriptures.

2. What are the New Rules of the New World?

The Laws of a New World (the laws of heaven)

The politic philosophy of a leader determines the social culture and ethics. Also, the philosophy of religion of a spiritual leader determines the social culture of the religious world. According to the scriptures of Korean new religions, now is the time of the Maitreya Buddha (Jeongdoryeong). Because the recording of predictions of Gyeokamyourok says that Jeongdoryeong finished the basic work of heaven and is ending to change the universe really. Due to the proclaiming of 5 covenants by the Victor in Korea, not only the weather but also the change speed of society, economy, and cultural environment are beyond of imagination. Humanity cannot recognize the authority of the Victor, there happen a lot of metaphysical mysteries. I gathered a lot of datum. Here are 5 covenants of the Victor. The Victor (the Maitreya Buddha=Jeongdoryeong) came to the world to change the mortal world into an immortal one. He is not a human but the Trinity God wearing a human's body. Here is his accomplishment for 33 years.

1) The Victor said, "I will remove communism."

First, He destroyed communism completely using His other selves by controlling Gorbachev in August, in 1991 according to the Seventh Angel's sayings and some proofs.

2) I will keep Korea from typhoons.

Second, He has stopped dozens of typhoons blowing toward the Korean peninsula.

3) I will stop rainy seasons.

Third, a rainy season of Korea is from 15 June to 15 July. In this season, rain fell down heavily and ceaselessly for one month for the past 3,000 years. But for the last 30 years it has disappeared since the advent of the Victor.

4) I will make Korean harvest abundant.
Fourth, Korean abundant harvest has been accomplished for 32 years since 1981.

5) I will Keep Korea from Korean Wars and Unify Korea
Due to the Victor's will, there are a lot of changes in the movement of Korean new religions. After the advent of the Victor, the existing religions were nervous because they preached interpreting the Bible by force just as the paradise is accomplished by their religions. Their researchers of Korean new religions interpreted their scriptures wrongly, and did not understand the true meaning of the words of their religion's founders. So they tell that the paradise will be built by their religions. However, when they are asked if the Sweet Dew falls in their religion or not, if there is a way of immortality in their religions, they cannot answer. I conclude that so far there was not the Victor of the scriptures in the Korean new religions. According to the predictions of the prophetic books, the Victor was supposed to appear in the late of twentieth century. So one should have found the secret of a new heaven in new new religions. They tried to find it in wrong places and mix and match their interpretations. This phenomenon is because they do not know the will of the Bible, their teaching was not perfect and gave up the aim of religions. They do not know how the work of heaven will be accomplished and finished, how the work of the Holy Spirit will be started and finished, and no one knows how to interpret the sealed secrets. I saw Christians deceive that the Victor's

five covenants are accomplished by Jesus in the subway train. Considering that people mix and match the words of God as those of the pseudo Savior, almost Korean new religions lost their role due to the ignorance of interpreting the scriptures and prophetic books and reveal their limit. Jeongdoryeong that emits the Sweet Dew tells that there was neither religion nor science. His sermons become more persuasive enough to change the mortal world into an immortal one. This is a real phenomenon of Korean new religion. I think that the immortal new religion will lead the Korean new religion and influence the world new religion riding Hanryu.

It is natural for new laws to be proclaimed in this era because the new heaven and the new earth are built. Next, I will examine the rules of the new heaven.

(1) What are the New Rules of the New World?

A common ultimate aim of Korean new religions is to build a new world without pain or death. The western new religions call this 'to build the paradise'. The point of advent of super humans (Theohumans) is when the new rules of the new era are proclaimed according to all the scriptures. The Bible calls the rule the Law of Liberty in James. The Law of Liberty is one that all humanity should keep, that is, rules of the mind. Those who keep the rules are qualified to go to heaven, so I name it rules of heaven. Therefore, a new rule of new heaven is one which was proclaimed by the Victor, all humanity should keep it.

(2) The Meaning of the Proclaiming of 'the Law of Liberty'

What is the Law of Liberty? It is a law that makes humanity not commit sins, makes them be reborn as the Holy Spirit. That is, it is a law that makes humanity live forever as God. Also, it makes heaven in people's mind by regarding everyone as my body.

Let me introduce the Law of Liberty. "Look at and adore the Reincarnated Maitreya Buddha, Victor, Savior who sends down the Sweet Dew every second." "Beat Self-Consciousness and kill it" "Regard the sins of brothers as mine." "Regard others' faults as mine." "Do not hate brothers" "Regard brothers' circumstances as mine."

"Regard others as mine" "Have the conviction of immortality." "Live a life in contrast of what Self-conscious desires" Conceive the mind of God all the time."

Next, I will tell the society of new heaven to be built by the Victor and neohumans. Neohumans are the men of heaven that are reborn as transcendent humans, attain eternal life, and are other existences to reinstate the light of God

(3) The Prediction of the New heaven and the new Earth and its Image of the Future

According to Revelation of the Bible, "Then I saw a new heaven and a new earth, for the first heaven and the first earth had passed away, and there was no longer any sea.

I saw the Holy City, the New Jerusalem, coming down out of heaven from God, prepared as a bride beautifully dressed for her husband. And I heard a loud voice from the throne saying, "Now the dwelling of God is with men, and he will live with them. They will be his people, and God himself will be with them and be their God.

He will wipe every tear from their eyes. There will be no more death or mourning or crying or pain, for the old order of things has passed away." He who was seated on the throne said, "I am making everything new!" Then he said, "Write this down, for these words are trustworthy and true." He said to me: "It is done. I am the Alpha and the Omega, the Beginning and the End. To him who is thirsty I will give to drink without cost from the spring of the water of life. He who overcomes will inherit all this, and I will be his God and he will be my son. But the cowardly, the unbelieving, the vile, the murderers, the sexually immoral, those who practice magic arts, the idolaters and all liars--their place will be in the fiery lake of burning sulfur. This is the second death."

One of the seven angels who had the seven bowls full of the seven last plagues came and said to me, "Come, I will show you the bride, the wife of the Lamb." And he carried me away in the Spirit to a mountain great and high, and showed me the Holy City, Jerusalem, coming down out of heaven from God. The wall of the city had twelve foundations, and on them were the names of the twelve apostles of the Lamb. I did not see a temple in the city, because the Lord God Almighty and the Lamb are its temple. The city does not need the sun or the moon to shine on it, for the glory of God gives it light, and the Lamb is its lamp. The nations will walk by its light, and the kings of the earth will bring their splendor into it. On no day will its gates ever be shut, for there will be no night there. The glory and honor of the nations will be brought into it.

(4) The Movement of a New Religion in 'the Victory Altar'

I studied Korean new religions and their scriptures' predictions 24 years ago. Especially I studied intensively a view of unique after life of the Victory Altar and the movement of its new religion. Because its followers usually earnestly sought the truth in Confucianism, Buddhism, and Christianity, and so on. They moved to the Victory Altar because they came to know their scriptures' predictions are realized in the Victory Altar. I came to know the fact while my participation observation method. This is a factor that I intuit that the movement of a new religion which occurred 30 years ago came to the final phrase. The Victory Altar insists that people go to heaven in a physical body, not heaven after death. Also they tell that spirit is body.

The new new religion shocked Korean new religions and has grown for 30 years. Among the existing Korean new religions, especially corrupted Christians oppressed the Victory Altar centering the Christian president of Korea. It disturbed the developing of Korean new new religions. The result of my study about the movement of the Victory Altar is giving a fresh shocking to the existing religions. Further the Maitreya(Jeongdoryeong, the Victor) is changing the world revealing the sealed secrets and manna, people are realizing them little by little. Also distorted facts by the mass media have been revealed one by one. Among them, a religion which reveals the essence of the Sweet Dew and explains the secrets of immortality logically and biblically is only the Victory Altar. The essence of the Sweet Dew is the most important factor that the world new religion should study because it is the material to save people from death.

(5) The new Movement of Saving Humanity by the Victor

Abovementioned the advent of the Victor and the movement of the Victory Altar is a new culture of saving dying lives, it is a new science. If religions are created to save humanity from death, the role of the existing religions which did not solve death is finished. Due to imperfect teaching and people who do not know the definition of religion, a lot of people died in 100 years' war, the war of roses, and so on in the name of the war of religion. Even now people kill innocent civilians in the name of the holy war. So there was neither religion nor science so far. A professor of Harvard University insists that the existing religions are useless. Also I felt there was neither religion nor philosophy when I was around ten years old looking at people did not live as their conscience and their scriptures' teaching. So I concentrated on the study of the scriptures and predictions about the future. Now I will introduce my thesis about the future culture of the paradise. So far, I examined the ultimate aim of Korean new religions and the rules of a new world. Also, I told about how the social structure and culture of the future would be. Unfortunately, theologians and philosophers do not know even the definition of religion and a meaning of existence of philosophy. Further as they are ignorant and lack of the passion to find out the truth and the essence of God, they do not know a fact that a new era is coming. The ultimate aim of the world new religion is to build the paradise. Now is the time one should know when and where heaven is accomplished through studying the scriptures and comprehensive research about the real phenomenon of new religions, we rethink what we should do. Considering that the Victor Jeongdoryeong of the Victory Altar points out the definition of religion definitely, I think that humanity has lived in darkness so far. Mr. Cho Hee Sung, the seventh angel who opened the seventh seal, told about the definition of science and religion as follows. "Religion is to realize the truth, the truth is to realize humanity and things neither to die nor to decay. Also knowing God that is the form of the truth is philosophy. Additionally to be reborn as God is religion. Defining the original of religion, if 'religion' starts with religio=bond, its origin word starts one Hananim=God, split into billions. Religion is to teach humanity to change their divided bodies into one body, that is, to reinstate God. Modern religion, theology, philosophy, and science consider humanity as an animal and insist groundlessly that they were created and evolved. However, Koreans have had the thought of 'Innaecheon' meaning 'humanity is originally God.' Also they have been taught that the root of humanity is God. Therefore, the predictions that new heaven is recovered in Korea, Jeongdoryeong appears with the Sweet Dew and builds new heaven are very natural. Also, the prophetic books predicted that the Victor would build the new heaven, emit the Sweet Dew, and be the hero of the Big Change. I already explained in my master's thesis in Mejiro graduated school in Japan. In the end, the efforts of neohumans to pioneer an immortal world will brighten the dark world. It will change the philosophy and religion of the world. Such a new cultural movement by neohumans will take an important role in changing of spirit of all humanity. It will get settled as a future culture of the paradise. I think that our duty is to be reborn as the Holy Spirit by studying the culture of neohumans.

CHAPTER IV
The Hidden Manna of New Heaven & New Paradigm of NRMs

 The purpose of this study is to reveal the secret of heaven's in the Bible, in the Buddhist scriptures, and in 「Gyeokamyourok(格菴遺錄)」, a Korean prophetic book. Also, I will focus on revealing the essence of the Sweet Dew(甘露) in the Buddhist Sutras and the Hidden Manna in the Bible. As well, the aim of my dissertation is suggesting the way that all humanity have no conflicts between religions and races. We have to become one to make a peaceful world. And it is meaningful to let the members of New New Religions rethink the true meaning of Salvation today, furthermore, to make all humans rethink where to go. The man who pours down the Hidden Manna is the Savior in the Bible, the Reincarnated Maitreya Buddha in the Buddhist scriptures(the Amrita Sutra, the Lotus Sutra, the Nirvana Sutra), and the Jeongdoryeong(正道靈) in the Korean prophetical Sacred Book, 「Gyeokamyourok(格菴遺錄)」 with 100percent accuracy. So Koreans are proud of it. Especially, viewing from the prophetic of 「Gyeokamyourok」, this the GamRo-HaeIn(甘露海印) and Holy Dew Spirit have become a key point to resolve the Salvation problem. The concept of Eternal life in 「Gyeokamyourok」 contains the meaning of immortality with a physical body. Also, the key point of this study is the new movements of Korean new religion to accomplish eternal life. Why? They have the same dream to pursue eternal life in this world in being alive, not going to heaven or the land of happiness after death. The reason New New Religious Movements and the waves of immortality happened in Korea is because the Hidden Manna predicted in all sacred books of the world has been revealed for thirty years. Nowadays, In fact, all religions of the world are jumbled up in Korea. Therefore, understanding new religions of Korea means understanding all religions of the world. To understand the New New Religions of Korea is the first step to know the Hidden Manna and Eternal life. Therefore, this paper is very important in the perspective to know the secret of the New Heaven.

1. A Study on the Secret of the Hidden Manna, GamRo-HaeIn(甘露海印)

The Secret of the Hidden Manna, KamRo-HaeIn(甘露海印)
The New Era is opened by the Hidden Manna

1) The Righteous Way and wrong paths

So far, there has not been found the way of leading to nirvana. A lot of pseudo religions have confused people and caused friction and conflicts with incomplete knowledge. False ministers like frogs in a small spring have led their followers to death saying "Here is a way(道), here is the truth, if you believe in somebody, and you will receive salvation." Are there real sciences, religions, and philosophies so far?

2) There are the Ways of leading to eternal life in the Scriptures

When you take a boat, you check first if there is not a hole.
Moreover, when you, the son of light, God, try to find the way of leading to happiness, the truth, or eternal life, you should think of it reflecting on the Scriptures and be led by them.
Now, a true teacher who teaches the way of leading to eternal life appears in Korea. In the 49th volume of Jeungilaham, the

Buddhist Scriptures, Sakyamuni said the Messiah (Reincarnated Maitreya Buddha) would appear in Silla country where king Gedu ruled. Silla is the country name of old Korea. According to Isaiah, a prophet, prophesied in the Bible that the messiah would appear at the corner, at the end of the land of the Far East. But the doubtful, ignorant, and acting out of self-interest Korean people did not know it also yet. There is an old saying that ignorance is the root of all evils. Those who are not wise do not know what the right path is, what they should know first to get the way of leading to eternal life.

How do they blindly want to lead to eternal life without finding out the way of leading to eternal life? Now is the time to get out of the way of leading to death; going to heaven after death, thinking of each other as others though all human beings are one. And we should find the way of leading to nirvana and complete ourselves.

3) The Sweet Dew is the spiritual food of New Heaven

The nature of Buddha 4-5 in the Grand Nirvana Sutra volume8, says what the nature of Buddha is. To conclude, the way of leading to nirvana is the Sweet Dew. When Sakyamuni was asked by his disciple, Gaseop, "What is the way of leading to nirvana", he answered, "the Reincarnated Maitreya Buddha's the Sweet Dew would save people" in the nature of Buddha 4-5 prophecy part the Nirvana Sutra Volume 8. So from the time when Reincarnated Maitreya Buddha comes and says the Sweet Dew, the era of the Maitreya Buddha's dharma begins and is completed. At that time of his death, he said after the Sweet Dew appears, the way of leading to eternal life would be completed. And the Sweet Dew is poured from the Reincarnated Maitreya Buddha, great nirvana, the Trinity Buddha, and amrita (amrita means the Dew Spirit in Sanskrit). Sakyamuni said that when he came as a connecting person between people and the Reincarnated Maitreya Buddha, he stressed when people believe the Nirvana Sutra, and they can meet the Reincarnated Buddha. Now, the law of the Sweet Dew appears in Korea. It is the time to throw away incomplete sayings and to teach the law of the Sweet Dew.

2. View on the Idea of the Messiah in Western Culture

1) What is the manna in the Bible?

What is the original meaning for manna in the Bible? Manna is a miracle food from heaven, according to the chapter of exodus (16:14-31) in the Bible, Number (11:6-9), Deuteronomy (8:3), Nehemiah(9:20-21), Psalm(78:23-24), John(6:31), the Epistles of St(9:2-4), and the chapter of Revelation(2:17). When Moses took the Israelites to the desert from Egypt, as there was no food with them, they almost starved to death. The people complained to him, therefore, he prayed to God. The Lord of God said, "You will eat meat fully in the evening, eat rice cake in the morning" In that evening, quails covered the camp place and the next morning, dew fell down densely on the ground, the dew disappeared and something white and round like frost piled there. Moses said to the people "God gave us this food; take the amount of food you can eat." This food has covered their camp site. They called that food manna. That food was like honey and snacks, as it disappeared, after sun-rise, they should gather it at dawn every morning. Also, as it was rotten after one day, they should bring the amount they could eat for one day; they were permitted 4 liters for each person. The Israel people lived on manna for forty years by them arriving to Canaan according to the Book of Exodus16:13, Number11: 6-9. Also, according to Epistle 9:2-4, one Omel(around three liter) of manna in golden pot in the Ark of the Covenant in the most holy place shows what the God fed on Israelites for forty years on the wilderness. The manna is not rotten and not changed. The Bedouins people of Israel call the manna food from heaven 'man as sama'. I think 'man as sama' is originated from mannu meaning food in old Egyptian and mann in Arabic which has the same meaning as food. In other words it can be defined as something coming from heaven. Also it can be defined as the symbol of food of heaven or food that Gods eat. What is the will of heaven that gave the manna to Israelites in Moses' period? John 6:31 revealed that Israelites would repeat the miracle of manna in the period of true Messiah. Christians treat Jesus as Messiah. However as he never corresponds with the Bible, it is non-biblical. Like the prophecy of Moses who saved the Israelites from hardships, the second Savior, the true Messiah should do the same as Moses. The man who saves dying people with the Hidden manna, the Holy Dew Spirit, is the true Savior and Messiah. If the manna of Moses' period is a physical manna, the Hidden manna in the Bible, in other words, the Holy Dew Spirit of the true Messiah is a spiritual food and manna that is the Holy Spirit, light. The Holy Dew Spirit in the Bible is the hidden manna of new heaven that makes all creatures dying in agony be reborn as the Holy Spirit and live forever in happiness. In Exodus 16:4-5 in the Bible, we can find the meaning of manna that it is bread as following this. Then the LORD said to Moses, "I will rain down bread from heaven for you. The people are to go out each day and gather enough for that day. In this way I will test them and see whether they will follow my instructions. On the sixth day they are to prepare what they bring in, and that is to be twice as much as they gather on the other days." The sayings hint that God will give humans the food of heaven in the future. The hidden manna of the new heaven is expressed as the GamRo-HaeIn(甘露海印=the Sweet Dew) 「Gyeokamyourok」. In Exodus 16:11-12, "The LORD said to Moses, "I have heard the grumbling of the Israelites. Tell them, 'At twilight you will eat meat, and in the morning you will be filled with bread. Then you will know that I am the LORD your God.' In this saying, bread is food, it also hints that God will pour down the hidden manna, the Sweet Dew, in the future. In Exodus 16:23-28, "Six days you are to gather it, but on the seventh day, the Sabbath, there will not be any." According to Exodus 16:26 in the Bible, "Nevertheless, some of the people went out on the seventh day to gather it, but they found none." This is the revelation of God through Moses that the Sabbath will be accomplished in the future. After God suggested that the seventh day is on the Sabbath, as one day is equivalent to 1000years in saying of the Bible, in the 7000 year, on the Sabbath will be accomplished. In the New Era, the food pouring down from the new heaven is not a physical world manna, but a spiritual manna, an immortal food, the spirit of God. That is, God will appear as the Savior to the world and will give a spiritual food, His Spirit, to people to save them. According to Hebrew 9:4 in the Bible, "this had the golden altar of incense and the gold-covered ark of the covenant. This ark contained the gold jar of manna, Aaron's staff that had budded, and the stone tablets of the covenant". This saying hints that the manna of heaven will not rot. Especially, according to Revelation 2:17 "He who has an ear, let him hear what the Spirit says to the churches. To him who overcomes, I will give some of the hidden manna. I will also give him a white stone with a new name written on it, known only to him who receives it." This saying predicts that the man who has the hidden manna will know the secret of the white stone and the name on it. He is the true Savior, Messiah, and the Victor.

2) What is the Difference between Moses' Manna and the Hidden manna
(1) The Manna of Moses

Israelites in Egypt who lived painfully as slaves escaped from Egypt by the leading of Moses. After that, they blamed Moses because of hunger; Moses prayed for food, God sent manna like dew. According to Exodus 16:4, the LORD said to Moses, "I will rain down bread from heaven for you." The people are to go out each and gather enough for that. In this way I will test them and see whether they will follow my instructions. (Exodus 16:13) That came and covered the camp, and in the morning there was a layer of dew around the camp. According to Exodus 16:15, when the Israelites saw it, they said to, "What is it?" For they did not know what it was. Moses said to them, "It is the bread the LORD has given you to eat." According to Numbers 11:8 "The people went around gathering it, and then ground it in a hand mill or crushed it in a mortar. They cooked it or made it into cakes. And it tasted like something made with olive oil." Like this, dew, that is, manna, fell down to the Israelis until they entered Canaan.

(2) The Sweet Dew and the hidden manna

The dew in the New Bible and the Old Bible is different. The dew in the Old Bible is a physical(肉)manna, the dew in the New Bible is a spiritual(靈)manna. According to John 6:49, "Your forefathers ate the manna in the desert, yet they died." According to John 6:27, "Do not work for food that spoils, but for food that endures to eternal, which the Son of Man will give you. On him God the Father has placed his seal of approval."

(3) The Manna which the Savior Pours down in the Victory Altar

According to Hosea 14:5, "I will be like the dew to Israel; he will blossom like a lily of Lebanon he will send down his roots"; Here, I is God because the sayings of the Bible is God's. Also Israel means victor. The name of 'Israel' was named to Jacob by God when he won an angel by the band of the Yappo river. Therefore, the descents of Jacob are called Israel people. Above mentioned words mean that the man who pours down the dew is the Victor as well as the Savior. because lily symbolizes the Savior. That is, the Victor is the Savior. Christianity sings like that in the chorus of 84th song of a hymnal. God is the Sweet Dew which the Savior pours down. According to Revelation 2:17, "He who has an ear, let him hear what the Spirit says to the churches. To him who overcomes, I will give some of the hidden manna". In those words, the hidden manna is the sweet dew as well as the spirit of God.

(4) What is the secret of a white stone and the Hidden Manna?

Like Revelation 2:17 in the Bible, the Victor said in 1990 that He received a white stone at the age of seven. He learned the word of 素砂(SOSA) in seodang(書堂=a private education institute before going to elementary school). He said that the name on the white stone is 素砂(SOSA)and he visited the place which is named 素砂(SOSA) when he grew up there. Like this, Israel, the Victor, is in the New Testament Bible, the Victor is the basis of Revelation. Revelation is the last part of the Bible volume 66, if the Victor appears, immortality, the aim of the Bible, is accomplished. Therefore God in John shouted the Victor to appear. Here what we should note is that the Victor, the Savior, and Israel. indicate one person(異稱). As God is the Alpha and the Omega, God of the beginning was reborn as God of consummation and became the Savior, and came to this world. The Bible is sayings of God, it was written by secret messages to avoid the attack from Satan. There is a pitiful circumstance of God in the Bible. The Savior is the man who was reborn as the Holy Spirit in Korea, the land in the Far East corner like the prediction of Isaiah. If a person receives the Holy Spirit, He knows the pitiful circumstance of heaven; He can reveal the sealed secrets in all the Scriptures in detail.

(5) The Sweet Dew is an immortal manna

Dew did not fall after Moses. Much later, Isaiah, a great prophet, predicted, "But your dead will live; their bodies will rise. You who dwell in the grave, wake up and shout for. Your dew is like the dew of the morning; the dew will give birth to her dead" in Isaiah 26:19. This predicted if the Savior who pours down the Sweet Dew appears, death would perish. The Sweet Dew is not a physical food, but a spiritual food. It means an immortal manna. Also according to 6:27, "Do not work for food that spoils, but for food that endures to eternal, which the Son of Man will give you. On him God the Father has placed his seal of approval."(1Corinthians 15:54) When the perishable has been clothed with the imperishable and the mortal with immortality, then the saying that is written will come true: "Death has been swallowed up in victory." According to Revelation 2:17, He who has an ear, let him hear what the Spirit says to the churches. To him who overcomes, I will give some of the hidden manna. I will also give him a white stone(白石) with a new name written on it, known only to him who receives it. Therefore, the word "humans' life-span is like trees'" is accomplished after the Holy Dew Spirit appears.

(6) The Secret of Visible Manna (Dew) in the Victory Altar

As the hidden manna that is poured down by the Victor is mystical, only a person whose spiritual eyes(靈眼)are opened can see the Sweet Dew. As God is the Holy Dew Spirit, the person whose mind is clean can see the Sweet Dew. 'Only the person whose mind is clean can see God. Also, the Savior is in the Victory Altar, the person who is becoming a righteous man can see the Sweet Dew in their naked eye. According to 2kings 6:17, And Elisha prayed, "O LORD, open his eyes so he may see." Then the LORD opened the servant's eyes, and he looked and saw the hills full of horses and chariots of fire all around Elisha. As the enemy came down toward him, Elisha prayed to the LORD, "Strike these people with blindness." So he struck them with blindness, as Elisha had asked. Elisha told them, "This is not the road and this is not the city. Follow me, and I will lead you to the man you are looking for." And he led them to Samaria. After they entered the city, Elisha said, "LORD, open the eyes of these men so they can see." Then the LORD opened their eyes and they looked, and there they were, inside Samaria. Sinners cannot see mystical things. If they regret their sins and remove Self-consciousness (我相), their spiritual eyes are opened and they can see the Sweet Dew. Today, there is nobody who says since cannot see the air, there is no air. What you cannot see exists. What you cannot hear exists in the universe. A lot of people who experience the Sweet Dew said that its taste is sweet, cool like peppermint, and ecstasy as the expression of the Bible. They feel their bodies become fresh and float. Also, they smell the strong scent of lilies that is fragrance of the Holy Dew Spirit. No matter how terribly people blame and defame the Savior, as he pours down the Sweet Dew, He is Jeongdoryeong, the true Savior. Like the prediction of 「Gyeokamyourok」, a Korean prophetic book, Korean Christians centering the Christian president enforced the Savior to go to jail from 1994 to 2000. 「GyeokamYourok writes "雙犬爭艸十口 暫時暫時不免厄" It means that Jeongdoryeong cannot avoid going to jail. It also says that the Savior is supposed to turn over the sinful dirty world and to recover the new holy world of God. Several scriptures record about the Sweet Dew. The Buddhist scriptures call the Sweet Dew Water,「Gyeokamyourok」calls the Sweet Dew(甘露), also it says people cannot die by eating it. The word of gamro(甘露) is interpreted as follows. gam(甘) means sweet and ro(露) means dew. The word of gamro(甘露) means sweet dew. And According to Exodus16:31, "The house of Israel named the manna; it was like coriander seed, white, and it tasted like wafers in honey." Although many religions have fought each other due to their different viewpoint, they were supposed to be united by the Savior. The Savior of all religions is one, that is, their leaders are not different persons. The Savior of all religions was supposed to come as one person. The man who pours down the Sweet Dew (甘露) is the true Savior.

3) What are the Essence of the Sweet Dew and the Mysterious virtue of the Holy Dew Spirit?

I narrated the origin of the term of the Sweet Dew and Holy Dew Spirit and the prophecy of Scriptures until now. Now I will tell the essence of the Sweet Dew and the Holy Dew Spirit and its effect to bodies through experiences. The grace of the Holy Dew

Spirit removes sins, agony, and sufferings. Therefore, people always enjoy happiness and joy; also the followers of the Victory Altar feel the phenomenon of getting young in the heaven. As well, the Holy Dew Spirit purifies the air as the air of Buddha by detoxifying through His other selves. As the air becomes that of heaven gradually, the new world that people do not need food to rot and they will live on the air is coming closer. The reason is because all the air will be changed into that of the Holy Dew Spirit. When sins in humans perish by the Sweet Dew, all religions are untied as one. Also there will be no quarrels in the world, and the world will become unified one unity. The time is coming new era by the neo-human who become Buddha, are saved, can fly first, then the time when all things and the universe are changed into light is supposed to come. The universe will be changed into an immortal one step by step as the Holy Dew Spirit is emitted by the Savior, the Reincarnated Maitreya Buddha. Prophetic books of Korea, China and the Buddhist books underlined that those who realized the true meaning and the essence of the Holy Dew Spirit should help the Victor(Savior) at the risk of their life. When the true Savior, the seventh angel, blows a trumpet at the last big changing phase of the Savior, the men who are accomplished fifty percent will be changed into light suddenly according to 1 Corinthians 15:51-4. People can see the power and essence of the Reincarnated Maitreya Buddha(the Savior) through His accomplishment of His five covenants. Although He came as a human's shape, as He has recovered the power of the Savior, God, He came as the fearful judge who works as His other selves and changes His body at will, but those who are indulged into desires and sins do not recognize Him.

4) The Mysterious Experiences of the Holy Saints in Pure Land (Spiritual Zion)

(1) The mysterious Sweet Dew affects to humans'-body as follows.

When the Fire Holy Spirit comes, people can smell the smell of burning paper. It is the smell burning decayed blood, in other words, sins. That is, if the Sweet Dew like fire comes to the bodies of the believers, their whole bodies become hot. When they devote more themselves to the Reincarnated Maitreya Buddha, they experience the grace of live water like cold water flows from the mouth to the abdomen. When people reach a higher step, they can smell the flagrance of the Sweet Dew like the smell of lilies, and their delusion and agony disappear, experience ecstasy, reach nirvana, and feel endless joy and delight. If people experience the Sweet Dew continually, their mind is purified, their bodies become light enough to fly, and they accomplish true heaven of heart being filled with peace. Each Scripture and prophetic book foretell as the Holy Dew Spirit that Mr. Cho Hee Sung, the Reincarnated Maitreya Buddha, pours out would shine infinitely, old people are changed into the bodies of sixteen years old in a moment.

When this experience occurs, if people take pictures, the pictures of the Sweet Dew are surely taken with forms of various lights. If people devote more themselves to cultivate, their bad characters are settled with those of God, and they accomplish mental peace. Those who have these experiences discharge dirty and decayed blood through urine and feces like coke color regardless of age or sex. These experiences are common phenomenon in the Victory Altar. No matter how serious the patients are, they are healed here through the experience of the Sweet Dew. Not only the phenomenon of old body getting younge, stopped menses starting, gray hair becoming black, but also several mysterious experiences make the Victory Altar different from the other religions where the Sweet Dew does not fall. Although the Sweet Dew makes old people with sixteens' younger bodies, the Holy Dew Spirit of the Savior does not go to everybody. It does not go to dirty bodies and dirty hearts. It goes to only clean bodies and hearts. Therefore as the Holy Dew Spirit stays at the men who have clean bodies and clean hearts. People cannot draw the Hidden Manna with their efforts without opening their mind. According to the Bible, "God will make the Victor be a column of a temple", God will give the hidden manna and a white stone to the Victor, and the white stone has name on it. The hidden manna never happened before in humanity being's history of 6000 years. In the period of Moses, when he took out the Israelites to the wilderness from Egypt and lived there for forty years, the people protested Moses to give food. Therefore, he prayed God to give them something to eat, and then manna fell down from the sky. The manna fell down and piled on the ground like snow. They lived on it every day carrying it in their baskets for forty years. Moses is the Savior because he saved the Israel people from Egypt. He said that the Lord, your God, will send you a prophet like me in the Act of Apostles. A prophet like Moses should pour out Dew to become the Savior like Moses. Moses saved the Israelites from Egypt; however, he was not the Savior who gives immortality, but the Savior who rescued from the slavery of Egyptians. Accordingly, the prophet like Moses means the Savior who gives eternal life to his people. As God is an immortal existence, when people go back to the original state of God, they become immortal ones. Humanity was originally God, and God exists in the blood of humanity as life. Humanity was made of their parents' blood, their parents were made of their grandparents' blood, their grandparents were made of great grandparents' blood. Therefore, the blood of God, the first ancestor, has been connected continually and it is here in humanity's, now. Accordingly, the saying that the blood of ancestors is in us today is very scientific. Satan wrote humans were made by soil to confuse them. However, humanity believes that the saying is that of God. It is very stupid. How can we make human body with soil? In fact that moment God was occupied by Satan, one half of God became God and the other half became Satan according to the Savior. That is the state of God nowadays: Neither is original God, nor is perfect Satan. Humans are in the middle of them. In order for humanity to be saved, they should go back to the original condition. So God can achieve salvation. In other words, men achieve salvation by becoming God, unless they become God, they cannot achieve immortality.

(2) The prediction and the proof of the Sweet Dew in the Buddhist Scriptures

The Buddhist Scriptures express the Sweet Dew(甘露)as the light of great nirvana that the Reincarnated Maitreya Buddha pours out, the whole Buddhist Scriptures such as, 大般涅槃經, 華嚴經, 楞嚴經, 法華經 write the Sweet Dew is the sign of the Reincarnated Maitreya Buddha. According to volume 26 of 華嚴經, the Reincarnated Maitreya Buddha can fill the universe with His other selves for an instance, removes the agonies of people. (分身遍照十方 甘露雨滅煩惱). The volume 5 四相品 of 大般涅槃經 says, "There are no death here because of the Sweet Dew(是處無死), the man who pours out this Sweet Dew is the man who reaches nirvana(無死即是甘露 是甘露者即眞解脫). According to volume 2 壽命品 of 大般涅槃經, Sakyamuni said for 48 years, "only when the dharma of the Sweet Dew comes, people would reach nirvana." When he was going to die without showing the Sweet Dew, his disciples crowded and asked Sakyamuni as follows: Buddha, we hope you to show and teach the dnarmc of the Sweet Dew to live long and not to die(唯願如來示導我等甘露正道 久住於世勿入涅槃). Judging the 壽命品 of 涅槃經 above, we can see that the Dharma of the Sweet Dew did not come yet at that time. Also, 如來性品 4-2, the volume 5 of 大般涅槃經 talked about the essence and the meaning of the origin of the word of the Sweet Dew concretely as follows: The Buddha is the existence that he or she neither delivers children nor dies, nor collapses, and nor takes diseases. It means nirvana. Death is not here. It is the Sweet Dew. This Sweet Dew is nirvana. In other words, it is the body of Dharma (法身). When a man dies, his body collapse, and his life perishes.

如來不生不滅 不老不死 不破不壞 無疾病者 卽眞解脫 眞解脫者卽是如來 如來無病
是故法身 死者名曰 身壞命終 是處無死 卽是甘露 是甘露者 卽眞解脫 如來成就 是功德

Like this the Scriptures said, the basic aim of the Dharma of the Buddhism is to get out of the cycle of birth and death, and to live forever enjoying ecstasy and happiness. Also, 法句經 安寧品 predicted if you want to be out of the cycle of birth and death of life(欲度生死苦 当服甘露味), you should receive the Sweet Dew.

(3) The hidden secret of heaven about the Sweet Dew in the Scriptures

Now I will examine the origin of the word of the Sweet Dew and the prediction in several Scriptures. The Betas Scripture of old India said the Sweet Dew is a heaven manna, Soma alcohol(天上酒) that gods drink. They call it the Sweet Dew because the taste is sweet like honey. Also the Buddhist scholars think the Sweet Dew is the alcohol of heaven, manna of heaven. As well it is known if people drink the immortal medicine of heaven (不死靈藥), the alcohol of gods, they will become light, God. Additionally, it is known as the mysterious heaven manna, which heals the agony of humans, makes them not age, and makes dead men come alive. Therefore, it is compared to the best taste, supreme level, the true way, and nirvana's synonym. The term of 'Amrta' implying such the Sweet Dew suggested when the Reincarnated Maitreya Buddha appears and talks about the right of the Sweet Dew, He would save all people.

(4) The hidden prediction of saints seeking the law of the Sweet Dew

First, Eunbiga(隱秘歌), the first part of 「Gyeokamyourok」says that the man who pours out the Sweet Dew is the Savior. Also, Haeinga((海印歌) of 「Gyeokamyourok」 predicts the Sweet Dew is the essence of elixir that the previous saints waited for and dreamed. And Doboosinin(桃符神人) part of 「Gyeokamyourok」 talks about the power of the Sweet Dew as follows: the mysterious Sweet Dew makes old gray useless men change into teenager's strong body, they never die and get old, and they stay as young men forever.

"白髮老軀無用者 仙風道骨更小年에 不老不衰永春으로 不可思議海印".
Also, we can see the effect of the Sweet Dew to humans in Sampunglon(三豊論) in the part of「Gyeokamyourok」. It says, in the first pung, the Sweet Dew makes bad men into good ones, in the second pung, the spirit becomes domicile, the third pung, the true Sweet Dew makes people reach nirvana. Suwoon(水雲) Choi Jewoo writes Podeokmoon((布德文) Dongkyeongdaejeon as follows: "Foolish people do not know the benefit of the Sweet Dew, they don't try to be changed(愚夫愚民 未知雨露之澤 知其無爲而化矣)" Also, Hwawoon((火雲), Kangjeungsan(姜甑山) predicts

in the part of the birth of the Reincarnated Maitreya Buddha chapter 81 of Junghwagyeong(中和経), his book, when the Reincarnated Maitreya Buddha appears, the Sweet Dew will fall down. On the day the Reincarnated Maitreya Buddha appears, the Sweet Dew will fall, at last people are open to Him, the men who are predestined to meet Him will realize after listening to Him. "佛日出時 降法雨露 世間眼目 今茲始開 有綠者 皆悉聞知" As well, Lao-ze says in chapter 32 Seongdeok(聖德) of Tao Te Chiang(道德経) "侯王 若能守之 万物 將自賓 天地相合 以降甘露 民莫之令 以自均" It means if emperors keep the way, all people will come. If the Sweet Dew falls down by heaven and ground being united, people become harmonious and follow them.

4) The Sweet Dew is a mysterious immortal material

The light of the Sweet Dew, the phenomenon of optical science and pure life, is a transcendent supernatural light which is impossible to explain with top-edge science. When this Sweet Dew stays at humans, it is like in the land of Perfect where the Reincarnated Maitreya Buddha and the Trinity Buddha stays, according to 如來性品 of the volume 8 in the Nirvana Sutra. The thousands pictures of the Holy Dew Spirit taken in the Victory Altar prove the prophecy of the Buddhist Scriptures about the true Reincarnated Maitreya Buddha. If people wash their heart continually, strong neutral light is emitted from them; this light is different from ordinary light. Actually one Korean emits the light strongly, the neutron light is not only the material of life and the light of God, is but also the light of Reincarnated Maitreya Buddha that kills demons in humans(殺魔光線). The light that the Reincarnated Maitreya Buddha emits is the material which makes immortality possible, when the immortal era is progressed whole heartedly, scientists will try to collect this material. However it is impossible. Because it is the light of the Savior, Reincarnated Maitreya Buddha, evil men cannot collect it. When people think of someone strongly, they can sense the smell of his mind. However they cannot usually notice the moving of the mind by the smell of men's mind. The men whose level of spirit reaches somewhat high can notice even others' delicate minds by their smell. All the scriptures foretell that all humans cannot but crowd to the Victory Altar where the Savior stays and is full of the Holy Sweet Dew to achieve salvation in the period of a big disaster. Also now is the time that all religion groups should realize that the Savior comes as the shape of the Sweet Dew, the Holy Dew Spirit.

3. A view on the Idea of the Maitreya in Oriental Culture

1) The Idea of the Maitreya Buddha in the Buddhist Scriptures

Through the study of Buddhism, Confucianism, Islam and many other religions, you might find out though the expressions are different, they all have the same teachings and doctrines. In Buddhism, they call the Savior 'Maitreya' who will appear in the future. The Maitreya means the Messiah and the Christ, the Christ is Israel, Israel is the Shiloh, the Shiloh is the Victor, and the Victor is the Victor God in the Bible. Well, the Maitreya Buddha is expected to appear in the year 3007 after Sakyamuni died on Buddhist Era (北方佛紀). 3007 B.E. Corresponds to A.D. 1980. The Buddhists also say, "to be a Buddha" people should be born again as the Holy Sweet Dew Spirit of the Future Buddha. And Maitreya means the Living Future Buddha who cures all the living from diseases and death with the Sweet Dew.

(1) Sukkavati (Paradise) is constructed by the Maitreya(彌勒佛)

未來世 佛出現時 國土所有 一切衆生 得壽命長

When the Living Future Buddha appears in the future, the span of life of every living thing in the world will be extended long.

有勢力獲大神通 衆生富足 所慾自恣 遠離貪淫恚癡

And every man will be possessed of supernatural powers. All creatures will live in opulence; will remove all desires such as avarice, a sexual desire, and stupidity.

常有花樹果樹香樹其中 衆生悉得清淨上妙音聲 常共和合

There will be always trees with flowers and fruits. Every man will have a clean and clear voice.

一切衆生共之 是名菩薩修淨佛土

And they will harmonize with each other because all living things are one being and Buddha. We call the Happy Land and Paradise.

昔所不得而今得之 昔所不見而今見之

You will get something which you could not get before.

昔所不聞而今聞之 昔所不到而今到之

You will hear something which you could not hear in the old times. You will reach anywhere which you could not reach in former times.

昔所不知而今知之 如來發明出世世法

You will know something which you could not know in the former times. The Living Future Buddha will teach the Dharma (law, truth) which will enlighten the world.

(2) The Authority of the Maitreya

知其本因隨所緣出 分身遍滿一切刹 放淨光明除世闇

He knows the essence of all living things and their causes and results. The other selves of Buddha can fill the universe. And it can remove the darkness of the world.

一念分身遍十方 窪甘露雨滅煩惱

Living Buddha's thoughts become His other selves and fill the universe. He pours out the Sweet Dew Water and it extinguishes the fire of anguish in man's heart.

一切衆生中最爲勝 一切聖人中最第一

The Victor is supreme among all living things, and all the saints.

假使百千無量諸魔 不能浸出如來身血 斷煩惱魔 陰魔死魔

No matter how much Satan can invade the body and blood of the Living Future Buddha, the Satan of anguish, adultery, death will disappear.

如來知身 金剛無壞

The body of Living Future Buddha will never perish like a diamond.

(3) What is the Sweet Dew(甘露)?

What is the true meaning of the Sweet Dew(甘露) and the Maitreya(彌勒佛)?

The Sweet Dew is Amrta(阿彌陀) in Sanskrit; it means elixir, a drink or medicine that gods drink. In India, they say that gods drink the Sweet Dew. When gods drink it, their agonies disappear and they are released from birth, aging, diseases, and death. Almost Scriptures speak of the Sweet Dew. Especially, the Beta Sutra of India says if people drinks the Sweet Dew, their bodies are changed into immortal ones and become light. Therefore, it is synonymous with best taste, highest level, and reaching nirvana. Also when the Maitreya(彌勒) comes, He pours out the Sweet Dew and save people according to almost Scripture, and it is a sign of the Maitreya Buddha (彌勒佛).

見佛聞法勤修行 如飲甘露心歡喜

If someone looks at the Future Buddha, listens to and practices His words, then he will drink the Sweet Dew water and be happy.

貪婬瞋恚愚癡 覆心 不知佛性

Because of desire, obscene acts, anger, and stupidity, no one recognize Buddha and the original nature of man.

血則變白 草血滅已

The blood will be changed into white, and decayed dirty blood will be removed.
Here, white blood means that of Buddha.
In the Sutra of Nirvana(大般涅槃經);

欲度生死苦 當服甘露味

If one wishes to escape from samsara (Rotation), he must drink the Sweet Dew Water.

無上甘露味 不生亦不死 (大般涅槃經 八卷).

It means that the Sweet Dew, highest taste, makes man not to die and not to be born.

三十三千上妙甘露 不死之藥 (大般涅槃經 六卷).

It means that the Sweet Dew, an heaven's manna, is the elixir of life, which makes man an immortal being.

是甘露者 卽眞解脫者 (大般涅槃經 五卷).

It means that the man who pours out the Sweet Dew is the man who has achieved liberation.

法性光明入毛孔者 必定當得 阿縟多羅三邈三菩提 (大般涅槃經 九卷 如來性品 4-6)

When the ray of the Sweet Dew permeates into the pores of a man's body, he will attain nirvana, that is to say, immortality.

(4) The Maitreya appeared in 15th Oct, 1980

知三千年後 名三世明燈 次知七日後 佛當出現 (華嚴經 70).

Three thousand and seven years after Sakyamuni has died, the Future Buddha will appear. The year of 3007 of the Buddhist Era is 1980.
The Victor Cho overcame Himself and became Buddha in 1980.

(5) The Maitreya emerged in Korea
將來之世 有佛名彌勒 出現於世 爾時國界名 鷄頭王所治處 (增一阿含經 49 卷)
In the future, Buddha will come out and be called the Future Buddha and the country where He will appear is ruled over by the king of Kaeud(鷄頭).
The king of Kaedu is a Korean king of the Shilla dynasty. Therefore, this means the Future Buddha will emerge in Korea.

(6) Maitreya's Surname is Cho(曺)
爲遭生老死苦者 飮以甘露 令其安隱 (華嚴經 78 卷)
(These are the words of Buddha in p.78 of the Avatamska Sutra.)
Cho(曺=the surname of Maitreya) will make people drink the Sweet Dew and reach Nirvana. Here, in the Avatamska Sutra, we can find Maitreya's family name. In other words, the Maitreya is destined to appear in Korea, from among the descendants of Cho.

曺還陽眞人始知天仙金丹大道 (華嚴經 78 卷)
Cho regained "Yang" (陽; the complete Buddhahood) and became a True Man, to make man immortal.

汝曺鬪時 瞋志恚毒盛珠陷入體故不自知 (大般涅槃經 七卷)
Until Cho has realized that the wicked devil is in man's body, no one will know that Satan is Ego.

喩如羝羊 是故名祖 (大般涅槃經 八卷)
Figuratively speaking, Future Buddha is like a ram. In other words, He is the progenitor of the human race. This means the zodiacal sign of the Future Buddha is the Ram, under which He was born. In fact, the Victor, Mr. Cho was born in the Year of the ram (羊, 辛未年生), 1931. And the Victor is the very one who recovered the Trinity God, Himself. Therefore, he is the pro-

genitor of the human race. Meanwhile, there is a mysterious thing connected with the Future Buddha in a temple in Korea. There is an old temple called Gaetaesa (開泰寺) temple near Nonsan, in the central south part of Korea. The temple was built by Wang, Keon(王建), the founder king of the Goryeo Dynasty(高麗王朝 A.D, 918-1392), who wanted prosperity and welfare for the nation. But, it was destroyed by fire when the Japanese invaded Korea in 1592, and rebuilt later. By the way, 19 years ago, when the Victor(the Maitreya) appeared, a strange thing happened, and it fell in Buddhist Era 3,000(1973).

There is a several hundred-year-old persimmon tree in Gaetaesa temple, and that tree has two thick branches. Between the two branches, a kalopanax tree grew, which has many thorns and leaves, in spite of there being no soil. Now, there are two kinds of trees and leaves on one tree, without graft into a stock. Gaetaesa temple has a legend that, if a kalopanax tree emerges between the persimmon tree branches, which would be a sign of the advent of the Future Buddha. And a persimmon tree(柿木) corresponds to the olive tree(the same pronunciation in Korea) which is the symbol of God. Therefore, the true meaning of a thorny kalopanax tree emerging between two persimmon branches is the proclaiming of the advent of the Future Buddha. According to Sakyamuni, udumbaras bloom once in 3000 years, when the Maitreya Buddha appears, it will bloom. The udumbaras of Urizul(Uri temple) proclaimed the advent of the Maitreya Buddha in Korea. In tradition, the thorny kalopanax tree has been used to dispel the evil spirit in Korea. So, that tree is the symbol of Victor killing the evil spirit, Satan, and re-building the New heaven and earth.

This has written in Buddhist Era 3,000(1973), The doorframe of entrance, Gaetaesa Temple(開泰寺)

4. The Advent of Jeongdoryeong is predicted in 「Gyeokamyourok」(格菴遺錄)
1) What is 格菴遺錄「Gyeokamyurok」?

 The predictions of 「Gyeokamyourok」 are superior to those of Michael de Nostradamus in accuracy. There are some prophetic books in Korea. Among them, Gyeokamyourok is a represen-

tative one. It was written Gyeokam(敬菴)or Gyeokam(格菴), Namsago(南師古) 450 years ago. It tells about Jeongdoryeong, a holy man from the offspring of Dan tribe. Jeongdoryeong means the man who rules the world with the right way, was supposed to appear in Korea in late 20th century and build an immortal world. Nowadays the book has been registered as 1495 ho in the old book list in Korean National Centering Library. So everybody can read it. It was sealed thoroughly by being written in broken Chinese letters, a metaphor; it is difficult for common people to interpret the whole book. So after the hero of the book appears, he can interpret it. For example, the perishing of the Yee -Dynasty, the attacking of Japan, the figures of modern Korea, the presidents of Korea, etc. were written 100 percent accurately 450 years ago. They could not understand it at that time. After the figures appear, they can interpret it. Another example is the term of Panmunjeom(板門店). The term was not at that time, neither was the place named by it. Because it was built after

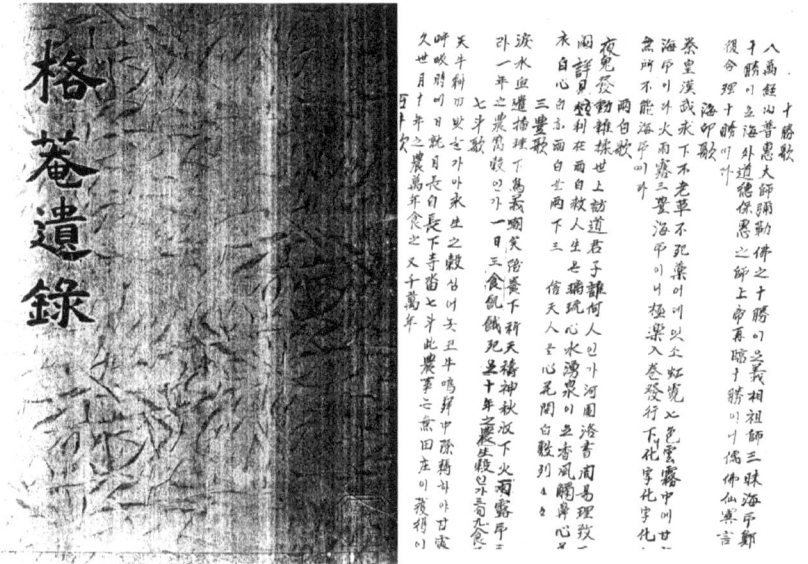

「Gyeokamyourok」(格菴遺錄)

Korean War in 1953. It is a name of village in the 38th parallel. So it was impossible to interpret it at that time. Therefore, after the hero appears, all prophecies are supposed to be interpreted by Him. It says exactly about Jeongdoryeong. The writer saw in advance that doubtful people would not believe the prophecy. So he prophesied all the figures and incidents of Korea with 100 percent accuracy. Also the book prophesied the advent of Jeongdoryeong exactly. The intention of the prophecy is to send a message to Koreans, which Jeongdoryeong will appear to build an immortal world. If He appears, do not hesitate to follow Him and enjoy immortality. In the year 1999, the seventh saint, the great King of horror, will come from heaven. The great King of the Monggols will bring to life. The famous French Prophet, Michael de Nostradamus, predicted that the Earth would perish in the seventh month of 1999. Moreover, Chapter 24 of Matthew and the Revelation of the Bible also have predicted a horrible future for Man and the Earth. The exhaustion of resources, the population explosion, the pollution and destruction of the environment; all these things make the future of Man gloomy. Cannot we have a bright future? Korea has a proverb "Just before the day-break, it's the most dark." Most of the teachings of religions and the great teachers of the world have postulated that all these bad situations can be reversed if mankind realizes its problems and tries to settle them. Returning to Nostradamus again, he predicted optimistically, "if other existence will appear in the East and take up his rule," all his prophecies and warnings could be postponed forever (Centuries 10:72), and that "the awaited help comes soon, yet too late" (Centuries 2:45).

 The Bible also predicts, "at the end of times, the Victor will appear and subdue the last enemy, death (1 Corinthians 15:26), and set up the New Jerusalem (Revelation 21:2), "Death shall be no longer, nor mourning, nor crying, nor any further pain" (Revelation 21:4). Now, communism, the greatest threat to man, has been rooted out completely by the Victor Christ. "He shall arbitrate the nations and shall decide disputes for many peoples; they shall beat their swords into plowshares and their spears into pruning shears; nation shall not lift up sword against nation, nor shall they learn war any more" (Isaiah 2:4). And "The wolf shall live with the leopard shall lie down beside the calf, the young lion, and the beef cattle together, and a little child shall lead them… and the weaned child shall reach its hand in the snake's nest"(Isaiah 11:6-8). Meanwhile, 「Gyeokamyourok」, the most accurate prophetic book from Korea, says that the Victor Christ will appear in Korea in late the 20th Century, in the name of Jeongdoryeong (正道靈; the King who will reign over the world with righteousness). It foretold the downfall of the Yi-Dynasty(Chosun; 朝鮮)

隆四七月 李花落 (格菴遺錄 末初歌)

The seventh month of 1910, according to the lunar calendar, a plum flower (the symbol of Chosun) will fall and the invention of the train,

 東北千里鐵馬行 (格菴遺錄 末初歌)

In the north-east, the iron horse will run 400 kilometers a day and predicted the telephone,

 無面相語萬國語 金絲千里人言來 (格菴遺錄 末初歌)

People will talk to one another without looking at faces, through a wire, words will travel a few thousand kilometers.
Here is a prediction of airplanes,

 空中行船風雲睫 赤旗如雨白鶴飛 (格菴遺錄 末初歌)

In the sky, a vessel will sail fast through the clouds; a white crane will fly like rain
and the defeat of Japan in World War II and the spread of the Sino- Japanese war into World War II.

 日本東出西山沒 日中之邊及於世界 (格菴遺錄 末初歌)

Japan (sun) rises in the east, and then sets in the west; the conflict between Japan and China will spread into a World War.
The date of the surrender of Japan is 14th August, 1945.

 青鷄七七 日力將衰 終亡之時也 (格菴遺錄 末初歌)

The 7th day of the seventh month according to the lunar calendar falls on 14th August, 1945. Besides these, it predicted the outbreak of the Korean war (Korean War, 1950) and it says the place of truce ; even the family names of ex-presidents, Lee, Seung-Man, Yoon Bo-Sun, Chun Doo-Hwan, and the president Roh Tae-Woo.

Above all, it prophesied the Advent of the Victor Christ (Jeong doryeongg in Korean), the unification of all the ideologies of the world, and the advent of the era of immortality. To begin with, I must talk about Jeongdoryeong (正道令).

2) The time and place of the advent of Jeongdoryeong(victor).

(1) The Victor's surname is predicted as Cho,(曺)

列邦諸人 緘口無言 大陸東方 海隅半島 人生秋收

糟米端風驅飛 糟飄風之人 弓乙十勝 (格菴遺錄 賽四十一)

Be silent! Nations and Islands, I will call a man from a peninsula (Korea) of the Far East, he (detach Mi (米;rice) from Cho (糟;bran) and that will be his Surname, Cho (曺)) will harvest flesh, and he is the very Messiah. This also agrees with Isaiah 41:1-9. "Silently listen to Me, You islands; ....

Who raised him up from the east? you whom I have taken hold of from the earth and called from its utmost corners, and ..."

(2) His first name is Hee-Seung

大白金星 曉星照, 欲識蒼生保命處 吉星照臨 眞十勝 (格菴遺錄 挑符神人)

The big white Venus shines. A person who seeks shelter, go to the bright star, who is Jeongdoryeong. Kum-Sung(金星) and Hyo-Sung(the morning star) and Gil-SUNG(吉星; the fortunate star) are the synonyms of Hee-Sung(the shining morning star). "I shall also give the Victor the morning star" (Revelation 2:28). He is the real Victor.

(3)The time of the advent of Jeongdoryeong

He began his mission on 18th August, 1981.

二十世紀後今時當 (格菴遺錄 生初之樂)

In the latter half of the 20th Century, Jeongdoryeong will appear. Born on the 28th day, 6th month, according to the lunar calendar of 1931, the year of the Lamb.

十五眞主 五未樂堂堂 靑龍之后 女上加一 狗驚 羊喜五十八年 (格菴遺錄 弓乙論)

In the year 1988, the persons who were born in the year of the Lamb (in the year 1931) shall be 58 years old, and will be happy.

In 1988, the Olympic Games were held in Seoul, and many visitors visited and learned about Korea. So, the Victor was happy. The Bible also symbolizes Christ as a Lamb. "A Lamb came and took the scroll from the right hand Him who was seated on the throne"(Revelation 5:7), "They will against the Lamb, and the Lamb will conquer them" (Revelation 17:14). "But the throne of God and of the Lamb shall be in it"(Revelation 22:3), etc. Therefore, Christ must be symbolized as a Lamb, and born in the year of the Lamb.

(4) Birth-place and of spiritual training

Jeongdoryeong, Cho, Hee-Sung was born in 1931, Kamjung-ri(坎井里), Kimpo-myun(金浦面), Kimpo-gun(金浦郡), Kyunggi-do(京畿道) in south Korea. In the beginning part(初章) of Gyeokamyourok, it has written as 漢水邊(the Han river side), 西湖出生眞人(出章論); Jeongdoryeong (眞人) will be born(出生) in Kimpo(西湖) which is located on the banks of the west side(西)Han River(漢水邊). Here, 西(the west) matches with 金(gold), according to the principle of the Five Elements, and 湖(lake) is a synonym of 浦(shore). Therefore, 西湖 is actually 金浦(Kimpo). The Bible also says, "Who raised him up from the east…, you whom I have taken hold of from the ends of the earth and called from its utmost corners" (Isaiah 41:1-9). Korea is located in the East from the European viewpoint, and is the end of Earth (because Korea is a peninsula), and Kimpo is the utmost corner of Earth, Korea.

In addition, Kam(坎) means a heaven or scoop, jung(井) means a well of life-water and ri(里) means a village. In short, the name of the village, Kamjung (坎井) means the drawing of water from the well of life-water with a scoop. That is to say, from this spring of the water of life, which is the very Victor, all the people of the world will scoop and quench their thirst with the water of life (Revelation 21:6).

And, he lived for about 30 years in Gyesoo-3ri(桂壽里)and Pumbakdong(範朴洞), where he was cultivated under his first spiritual master, 靈母, Youngmonym (the spiritual mother, that is the Elder teacher, Park, Tae-Sun). and then he blessed at the place, which heaven and earth hide, that is Gyesoo(桂壽) and Pumbak(範朴).

(5) Prediction of the actual chamber

And he cultivated the providence of salvation for the whole of mankind under his second spiritual teacher, Victress Eve, in Milshill (密室 means the hidden house or chambers in Isaiah 26:20) during the period 1978-1980, and obtained permission as Victor from God on the 15th October 1980.

蘇萊老姑兩山相望稀座 (格菴遺錄 聖山尋路)

Here is located between Mt. Sorae(蘇萊) and Mt. Nogoh(老姑).

隱居密室生活計 (格菴遺錄 末運論)

He hides himself in the hidden place and cultivates plans for the salvation of mankind.

① Milshill (密室) is the actual chamber

Mt. Sorae(left) and Milsill(密室); the actual chamber

"Go, my people, enter your chambers, and lock your doors behind you. Hide yourselves a little moment until the indignation is passes"(Isaiah26:20). God's indignation means the war between the angels dragon (Revelation 12:1-9). This also accords with 12:1-9 of Revelation. He ("a son, a male child, destined to rule all nations with an iron rod") was cared for by the Victress, Eve("a woman, robed with the sun, with the moon under the feet and crown of 12 stars on her head was pregnant, fled into the wilderness during the battle between Michael and his angels against the dragon") for 3 years (1978-1980).

② Prediction of the starting place on the new earth
He established the Victory Alter in Sosa (素砂), the name of the place where the Victory Altar is located means a white stone. 「Gyeokamyourok」 says that 始終艮野素砂地 (格菴遺錄 末運論). It means that I(God) will begin and finish my work in Sosa.

武陵桃源, 天崩地柝素砂立 (格菴遺錄 出將論)

Sosa is Paradise. Although the Garden of Eden was lost 6000 years ago, it will be set up again Sosa (the white stone). "To the Victor I shall give a white stone, and engraved on the stone will be a new name, which no one knows except the recipient" (Revelation 2:17).

(6) The Symbol of Jeongdoryeong (=Victor)

東海三神不死藥 甘露海印 (格菴遺錄 弓乙圖歌)

The elixir of Mt. Samain in the East sea is the Sweet Dew.

秦皇漢武求下 不老草 不死藥 甘露如雨海印 (格菴遺錄 海印歌)

The cure-all, which the old Chinese emperors sought, is the Sweet Dew. The symbol of Messiah is Dew. According to Hosea 14:5, "I will be the dew to Israel (Victor in Hebrew); he shall blossom as the lily". Lily means Christ, according to a Hymn. "But Thy dead shall live, including my corpse; they shall rise. You who dwell in the dust awake and sing joyfully; for Thy dew is a dew of light, and Thou shalt drop it on earth, upon the dead" (Isaiah 26:19).

火雨露三豊海印 極樂立券 (格菴遺錄 海印歌)

I will give signs in the heavens and upon the earth, blood and fire, and columns of smoke"(Joel 2:28-30). And they are the tickets to Heaven.

(7) Unification of All the Religions by Jeongdoryeong

The true Teacher (Shepherd) of all mankind must have the authority and ability to unify all the religions and ideologies into one Truth.

「Gyeokamyourok」 writes 儒佛仙 異言之說 末復合理十勝 (格菴乳錄 十勝歌)

The doctrines of Confucianism, Buddhism, Taoism, and Christianity are different, but, at the end of time, all their doctrines are unified into one truth, that is to say, the teaching of Jeongdoryeong; "Man was God and must become God."

For example;

    八萬經內普惠大師 彌勒佛之十勝이요 (格菴遺錄 十勝歌)

The Maitreya in the Buddhist Sutras is Jeongdoryeong.

    海外道德 保惠之師 上帝再臨十勝이다. (格菴遺錄 十勝歌)

The comforter, the spirit of Truth in the Bible is actually Jeongdoryeong.

    三家三道末運 一仙之造化蓮花世 (格菴遺錄 隱秘歌)

The three major religions, Confucianism, Buddhism, and According to Christianity will be unified into one religion and construct the Paradise on this Earth. According to Isaiah 2:2, "It shall be in the latter days that the mountain of the Lord's house shall be firmly established as the highest of the mountains and be raised above the hills, to which all the nations shall stream."

(8) 「Gyeokamyourok」(格菴遺錄) predicted the New Era of Immortality

「Gyeokamyourok」(格菴遺錄) prophesied that an era when man would become young and never taste death would appear.

    白髮老軀無用者家 仙風道骨 更小年 二八靑春妙 態度 不老不衰迎春化

    (格菴遺錄 桃符神人)

"The old man with white hair becomes young, his body is also changed into a youth's, and he never grows old and maintains always vigor." According to 1 Corinthians 15:54-55, "And when this perishable has put on imperishability and this mortal has put on immortality...," then, Death is swallowed up in Victory. Death! Where is your Victory? Death! Where is your sting?"
「Gyeokamyourok」(格菴遺錄) predicted that a foolish man could not enter the Kingdom of God. It records as follows.

 愚者信去天堂人 今時滿員不入矣 終身愚人地獄 (格菴遺錄 嘲笑歌)

Oh! The foolish are those who believe in God and think that they can enter Heaven. By this time, Heaven might be overcrowded. Your final fate (destiny) is Hell!
In the Bible, in Luke 17:20-21, it says "The Kingdom of God does not come by looking for it, neither will they say, 'Look! Here it is,' or 'There it is!' For the Kingdom of God is in your midst" And it also criticizes Confucianism, Buddhism, and Christianity, in fact, all of the religions of the world.

 孔孟讀書稱士子 見不覺無用日

All the students of Confucius and Mencius! All of you say, as it were, that you are the disciples of them. But you are ignorant and foolish unless you do not just see, but realize.

 阿彌陀佛道僧任, 念佛多誦無用日

All Buddhist priests!
You only recite all the sutra, and waste away days and time.

 彌勒出世世何人覺

But who can know that the Maitreya has already appeared.

 海外信天先定人 唯我獨尊信天任 降大福不受 (格菴遺錄 精覺歌)

You, Christians! Who believe that your exclusive privilege to enter Heaven was appointed before the creation? You cannot receive the great blessing from God.
「Gyeokamyourok」(格菴遺錄) writes that humanity is God again.

自心天主, 人心卽天 (格菴遺錄 格菴歌辭)
God is in man's mind; therefore, the mind of man is the very Kingdom of God.
And 「Gyeokamyourok」(格菴遺錄) teaches us to regard every one as ourselves:
愛隣如已 (格菴遺錄 末初歌) it means, "Regard everyone as ourselves." At any rate, all the religions and the great masters have expressed the same meaning in various ways. But, so far, people have believed that God is different from Maitreya, and Christ is different from Victor. As a matter of fact, the Victory God is Christ Messiah, Messiah Victor(Israel), Victor is Jeongdoryeong, and Jeongdoryeong is just Shiloh. According to the Victor, there has been no true religion or true learning in the world, so far. True religion must be realized within man and, when man becomes God, an immortal being, then. We can say that we have religion or truth. The aim of religion is that it makes man immortal. Here is a hymn of the Victory Altar to praise the Holy Dew Spirit
'The Holy Dew Spirit'

1.The rainbow - colored Holy Dew Spirit is shining brilliantly,
This is the Holy Spirit that all humanity has waited for 6000 years.
Because He appeared in this land to save anguish people,
Mountains, brook, grasses, and trees danced and all things are happy.
Let's praise the light of eternal, the light of life,
Let's praise the light of salvation, the light of light..

2.The Holy Dew Spirit of God that is the shape of blood, fire, and a pillar of smoke,

He came to this land to save the people of heaven,
He leads to heaven by saving people wandering people who are in the way of hardships and thorny.
Let's praise the light of eternal, the light of life,
Let's praise the light of salvation, the light of light.

3. The Dharma light of the Maitreya Buddha that is shinier than the morning star,
As He illuminates the dark world, the universe is bright
108 anguishes perish, agony and illusions disappear,
We are deeply moved, our heart is full, and the world of nirvana is here.
Let's praise the light of eternal, the light of life,
Let's praise the light of salvation, the light of light.

4. The water of life washes away the dirty sin of the world of red dusts,
The Holy Dew Spirit burns the sins ingrained with greed,
The Dew of the Lord is brilliant one, which is full of the universe
The heaven is here that smells lilies and the Sweet Dew.
Let's praise the light of eternal, the light of life,
Let's praise the light of salvation, the light of life.

2. The New Theory of Immortality through the Principle of Blood
1) The Principle of blood
The law of nature is the law of heredity, and the law of heredity is the law of blood. So the monkey bears a monkey, the hare bears a hare, and the cow bears a cow. Likewise, human being gives birth to a human being. Therefore, all creatures have their

own blood proper to their species. On this, it is truth of man's blood that man can be a man. Meanwhile, blood can't be made even by modern top-science. Only God can make blood. Therefore, the mystery of blood is the mystery of creation, and the mystery of creation is the mystery of nature and cosmos. Therefore, if we can solve the mystery of blood, we shall come to know the mystery of all and everything.

(1) The Unity of Spirit and Body

Most People think that body is one thing and spirit is another. What is more, many people even think that spirit and soul are different from each other. Such distinction between spirit and body, spirit and soul has been the foundation of religion and science for thousand years. But the idea of the separation between spirit and body, and the discrimination between spirit and soul are neither Biblical nor scientific. All such inheritances are nothing but dream and fantasy. Because a human mental structure can project anything through its imagination whatever it may be, such false hypothesis have been established and accepted for thousands years. But in fact, spirit and body cannot be separated apart. They cannot exist independently also. They are rather one. As for spirit and soul, the spirit is the thinking process or mind itself, and the soul is the thinker or experiencer who controls his thoughts. Therefore, the spirit is in the soul, and the soul is in the spirit. They cannot exist apart. Therefore, spirit and soul are inseparable each other. They are the same thing. That is to say, soul is also thought, like spirit is.
BLOOD= LIFE= CELLS= HEART= BODY= SPIRIT
Blood= Cells= Body
Cells are formed of blood, flesh and bone are formed by the cells. So cells, flesh, bone, and body are nothing but the extension of

blood. They are all blood itself. Cells are blood, flesh and the body are blood. Also, even hair, fingernail, and toenail are all blood itself. On this, the Koreans call a newborn baby "Pit-tungee" (=a lump of blood).

Life= Heart= Spirit

Man happens to faint or sometimes to die from astonishment or shock. Man can be killed also by hypnotism. These facts suggest that heart (=mind) and life are inseparable from each other. As the Bible says that the heart is the source of life (Proverbs4:23). Therefore, the heart is in life and the life in the heart. That is to say, life is just heart and the heart is just life (Psalms31:30). On the one hand, a body without life has not the heart. The body without life is the dead. There is no such thing as spirit or mind in the dead. So the life and the spirit are inseparable. They are the same one. The life is the spirit and the spirit is the life (Genesis2:7).

On the other hand, we call a thinking man a spiritual being. It suggests that thought is just the spirit. And now thought, mind and spirit are nothing but synonyms. They all indicate the same thing, which is human heart. Therefore, the heart is the mind, and the mind is the spirit(1 John4:6), and the spirit is the life (James2:26), and the life is the heart(Psalm31:10).

Blood= Life= Heart

If man is short of blood, he will have anemia. If man sheds blood too much, he may die. If a beast's blood is transfused into a human blood-vessel, the man will die at once. The man happens to die from the heart failure. These facts suggest that blood is the source of life. On this, many idioms such as "to the last drop of one's blood" or "give one's blood for one's country" or "have A's blood on B's head" demonstrate also that blood is just the life

(Gen9:4). And in fact, all activities of life such as breathing, secreting, digesting and sensing are performed by blood. So the Bible says that blood is life (Lev17:14, Dt12:23). Meanwhile, human disposition or temper is different according to blood types. The man of type A is meticulous and careful. The man of type B is obedient and sociable. The man of type O is violent and radical. These facts suggest that human mind is just the working of blood. On this, we call the pump not "the pouch of blood" but "heart". And now the pump pulses differently according to various circumstances. It pulses fast when you get angry. It pulses clam when you sit down and relax yourself. These facts indicate that blood, body, and heart are inseparable. Therefore blood is the heart, the heart is the life, and the life is blood.

Body= Blood= Spirit

As we have seen so far, blood is life and heart, and heart is spirit. Consequently, blood is just spirit. On the one hand, blood is cell, cells are flesh and bone, and flesh and bone are the body. So blood is just the body. Therefore, spirit is body, and body is spirit. Nevertheless, most people have the idea that body is one thing and spirit is another. This mistaken idea is due to the inferior and imperfect religion which wos born false witness. But as we have seen above, spirit and body can never be separable apart. This truth is Biblical and scientific. And in fact, human's thought is the working of nervous system. Nerve-cells are spreading over the body. Through such nerve-system, man can feel and think. That is to say, the whole body is the spirit, as it is. Therefore, it is a groundless lying that man's spirit enters the kingdom of heaven after his death. When you die, you body-dies actually. Your spirit or soul dies also like your body. Therefore it is a terrible lie that one's spirit or soul enters another world such as the kingdom of God or the abode of the spirit after his death. As the Bible has it, man dies and enters the hell for the wages of sin (Ro6:23, Jacob1:15). Accordingly, anyone who dies enters the hell. As for the kingdom of God, however, the kingdom of God is where God lives. Now the Bible says that God lives in our hearts (1Corinthians3:16). Therefore only those who live eternally with their bodies (=hearts) deserve coming in the kingdom of God. Many people think that God is one thing and the kingdom of God is another. But it is not true. Because the Bible is a spiritual book, the whole Bible express a human mind. The Valley of Baca expresses human's mind (Psalm84:6), and the desert, the parched land, the wilderness, the blind, the ears of the deaf, the tongue of the dumb, streams in the desert, all express human's mind (Isaiah35:1-10). And the war of Armageddon expresses the war of mind (Revelation16:16), and the book of life (Rev17:8), the water of life (Rev21:6), the tree of life (Rev2:7), the hidden manna (Rev2:17), and all express human mind. Babylon (Rev18:2)also express, "the new heaven and the new earth (Rev21:1)are human's mind." Similarly the Abyss or Satan (Rev17:8) expresses human's mind, and the kingdom of heaven or God also expresses human's mind. That is to say, Satan is just the hell of mind, and God is just the paradise of mind. So the Bible says, "Blessed are they who know their spiritual poverty, for theirs is the kingdom of heaven... Blessed are the pure in heart, for they shall see God (Matthew5:3-8)" The spiritual poverty means the empty mind and the pure in heart indicate those who are not disturbed with worldly thoughts. As we have seen so far, the kingdom of heaven is right in our heart. Therefore, only those who are alive deserve to enter in the kingdom of heaven.

The Identity of God and Human

The whole mankind was the blind. Though God was in front of them, they could not see him. All that they could do was to mutter God invisible. But the Bible says precisely that human being is just God. Nevertheless, no one could dig out this truth from the Bible. Most clergymen or theologians used to insist that the imaginary God was in heaven. Therefore, they were the blind leading the blind, and their preach or theology was a kind of blind man's buff. But the Victor in the Victory Altar, he has revealed all to the world and opened our eyes to the truth. So we come to know the temple where God dwells. Furthermore we come to see God face to face whenever and everywhere.

2) The New Theory of Immortality through the Principle of Blood

Everybody wanting to live forever is the nature of humans. Everybody wants to live long without dying, that is the nature of humans. Although there is another world after death, even faithful believers or babies who know nothing are afraid of death. Death is a pain of pains and the root of all panics. Why? Because, first, they have conviction that another world does not exist after death. Second, death is not the nature of humans. Considering this view, death is never the end station of humans to go. Nevertheless, why humans surely die? First, we should know the reason of humans' death in order to find out the immortal secret. So far, nobody clearly said the theory of immortality medically. Mr. Cho Hee-Sung, the Seventh Angel according to the Bible, reveals it for the first time. Humans are God that is the essence of eternal life. While I studied the philosophy of immortality, I was able to see that Mr. Cho Hee Sung preaches the methodology and new theory that humans are reborn as God and changed into light of immortal life.

(1) The reason of aging and death is revealed through the principle of blood

Most religious doctrines are superficially reflected by the hope of humans' twisted immortality. The theory of separating body and spirit, separating God and humanity form this world, believing heaven and hell after death, and the samsara of spirit are the products of the twisted thought. These religious thoughts are just reflected by illusionary copies of the natures that are embedded in our blood. Most of all, the prophets who a lot of religionists revere look like faded idols to the followers of the Victory Altar in the era when the Sweet Dew falls down. Although existing religions know neither the essence of sins nor the secret of beginning that has been recorded in blood and has come down through blood and lineage, furthermore, they do not know the principle of blood exactly, they have lead their religions in their thought for thousands years.

(A) People do not die because of aging

People die due to several reasons such as accidents, diseases, hunger, cold, aging, etc. Among the reasons, most people die of natural death due to aging. Most people think that people die because of aging. Is this saying truth? No, it is not. According to the preaching of the Seventh Angel, people die not because of aging, but some causes of death. Therefore, a lot of scientists have studied the reason of aging. They have not found out the reasons yet. According to the Bible, people die because of the wage of sins. According to the Nirvana Sutra, the Reincarnated Maitreya Buddha appears and preaches "The Blood of people is decayed, they cannot attain the nature of Buddha, and they die. However, they do not believe the saying of the Reincarnate Maitreya Buddha." The Seventh Angel revealed the secret in Buddhist Scriptures on the platform of the Victory Altar. Although all religious Scriptures speak of immortality with physical bodies (不死永生), people who are caught by karma do not believe it. Most people think that humans' death as natural. On the contrary the followers with spiritual eyes of the Victory Altar know that Scriptures predicted when, where, and how eternal life would be established. They insist strongly that they should announce that people can achieve eternal life with physical bodies. Also they say that people should not distort the essence of prophets' predictions. Especially, the Bible says when the Messiah comes to the world; people will be able to accomplish immortality. According to John 5:39 says, "You study the Scriptures, because you think that in them you will find eternal life" According to Titus 1:2, "God promised eternal life to His chosen people before the beginning of time." According to 1Corinthians 15:26, "The last enemy to be defeated will be death." "Where the Sweet fall down, there is not death" according to the Nirvana Sutra. The Scriptures speak of eternal life with living bodies. If people die because of aging, they should grow old at the same rate, die at the same time and in the same conditions. However, there are big differences in aging regardless of age. Then, where is aging and the cause of contracting diseases? Let's find out the real reason of death and aging from the view of the theory of Immortality.

(B) The causes of aging and the essence of spirit

There are several medical and biological theories about aging. For example, they are 'the theory of mutation', 'the theory of autoimmune' saying that aging comes from the immune system's weakening, and 'the theory of circulation's disorders, etc. However, they did not say the reason of aging exactly. The modern medical world says that aging comes from reducing the activity of cells. However, their explanation about the reason of death and aging is not clear. According to the theory of the Seventh Angel, because Self-consciousness that is the root of desires works, people's blood is decayed, as the decayed blood increases gradually, reformed cells decrease. So the phenomenon of shortage of cells occurs on the whole body, not because they become old by growing old. Cells have their life-span, after finishing their life span, they die. Then new cells are formed by not decayed blood. So if blood is decayed, the shortage of cells occurs. Therefore, increasing the amount of decayed blood, black spots are formed gradually on their faces, germs occurs in their blood, the resistance of white blood cells gets weak, finally they contract serious diseases, and die in the end. In other words, according to the principle of blood, people's blood is decayed, and the decayed blood does not form cells, the shortage of cells occurs, so their skins have wrinkles gradually. Living people are like tombs of dead people's spirits, which are filled with good deeds(善業) and sins. The spirit (blood) of my dead ancestors exists in my body in this world today. If the ancestor of humans was immortal God, as the working of the blood that composes my body and mind is equivalent with that of the mind. As people' body and mind were formed by the blood of their ancestors, people's bodies are transformed by spiritual body of God and they are imperfect gods and caught in Satan's prison. Those who have a lot of sins take death for granted by the memory of genetics of decayed blood and the information that the soul of death gives, also because of minds such as desire, anger, sadness, and so forth that kill humanity's life, people become old and die. That is the new theory of Neo-humans about the reason of death.

(C) The reason of contracting diseases and traffic accidents

The Seventh Angel tells that the reason of people's death from car accidents is because they are shocked at the moment of car accidents. Those who have a lot of decayed blood are startled easily. Also, having a lot of decayed blood means that they have much of the soul of Satan. When people do a blood test, some people have dark blood, others have scarlet blood. Those who have scarlet blood are not usually surprised but those who have dark blood are surprised easily. The Savior has difficulty giving them grace. No matter how strongly the Savior gives grace to the followers, it is difficult for those who have a lot of sins to receive the grace of God. Such people should make efforts to receive grace with an opening mind every day to make blood clean. Then their minds change and feel peaceful. If people's blood gets clean, their minds become new as much as their blood becomes clean. Their bodies become light as much as their blood becomes clean. They become healthy, and they can live forever according to the Seventh Angel. Deepak Chopra who is well known as a medical doctor said through 『Men do not grow old』 that "the speed of aging, contracting disease, and dying is not due to age in aspect of alternative medicine." When people worry about something or attempt desires, their blood is decayed and germs occur in the decayed blood. The reason of contracting diseases and aging basically results from the working of mind that decays blood, the working of mind influences strongly the changing of blood. The believers of the Victory Altar learn the principle of blood every day in order to get out of the cycle of birth and death through the Seventh Angel's preaches. They receive the Sweet Dew that makes blood clean every day, listen to the science of immortality through worship services, practice the philosophy of one body and the Law of Liberty, and have the mind "considering everybody as my body" that makes people be reborn as the Holy Spirit. Then I will introduce the theory of principle that spirit and body are one and the Sweet Dew that is the medicine of immortality.

3) The principle of immortality

There is an old saying in Korea; "If you know, you escape from death." This saying is usually cited as the saying of prediction if you know the secret of immortality, you can escape from death. People's aging and dying is not due to age, but blood being decayed. Germs generate in decayed blood, as the decayed blood cannot form new cells, it causes the shortage of cells and aging is progressive. The most influential factor that makes people's blood decayed is attempting desires. Now, I will address what is 'the fundamental root of desires', the way of removing 'I', Self-Consciousness, and which makes people attempt desires. Also, to be reborn as immortal bodies, people should know exactly how desires and illusions that cause agonies affect bodies, the relationship between blood and life, bodies and mind, the whereabouts of sins, and the root of life.

Mr. Cho Hee-Sung, the Seventh Angel, preached that the working of blood is that of mind, blood itself is the mind, blood itself is the spirit. As people's flesh and bodies are formed by their blood, their bodies are their spirit. Also, thinking determines humans' fate and lifespan; it makes eternal life possible. That is the principle of blood and the secret of immortality. Because the root of good and evil lie in blood and sin is in blood, purifying blood is the fundamental solution for immortality.

Also people's minds which have a close relationship with blood determine to go to death or to enjoy eternal life.

(1) Blood is just life

As life lies in blood, the behavior and mind making blood decayed is killing life. The Bible express that blood is life in Genesis 9:4, Leviticus17:11. It is common sense that almost all patients dying from excessive bleeding come to life again if they receive a blood transfusion. That is verified in the medical world that blood is life. Humans' fetus is formed through the division of cells which each have genetic information from one drop of their parents' blood. A humans' body is formed by 100 trillion cells. As cells cannot last forever, each cell has a different lifespan. The cells of skin live for twenty-eight days, some cells of hormones can live for only a few hours, and the cells of bone live for eight years. Therefore, several hundred million's cells die a day and are discharged. And new cells refill, only clean blood can form new cells. For example, if 100 cells die, if their blood is 100 percent clean, 100 cells are made. Aging does not exist anymore. However, almost all people attempt desires in their lives, therefore, their blood decays. as decayed blood does not make new cells, aging happens to people. That is, if a man's 100 cells die, as his blood decays twenty percent, eighty new cells are formed. As a result, the shortage of cells happens. It makes wrinkles, and the whole body comes to lose its power and its functions gradually. The shortage of cells reduces the number of white blood cells, so his body loses the power to overcome germs, comes to death finally. It says how important blood is. Then, is there a way that blood is not decayed? That is, the way to live forever? That is the duty of the science of immortality. If blood is life, what is the root of life? All religions and the Scriptures say that life is just God. So all of them commonly have religious precepts that they prohibit to kill life and not to eat the meat with living blood. Death is the phenomenon when people's blood is decayed 100 percent or they excessively bleed. In other words, death means God, life, dies and perishes. Therefore, to know the root of life is the shortcut to understand the principle of immortality

(2) The root of life is God

All living things emit the light energy of life. Modern physicists have already said that atoms compose all materials. Neutrons are in the nucleus of atom, and negative electrons go around the nucleus. The power of making the negative electrons go around the neutron is not automatic, but due to the power of life. Having the power of life is being alive, being alive means having life. On the other hand, dying is losing life. If the essence of life is God, the essence of death is Satan, the soul of devil. Then what is life? Life is just God. Satan, the soul of devil, has no life; it has only the soul of death. The soul of death rides God and kills it in the end. Therefore, humans death means that God that is the root of life dies and the light energy of God that is immortal living things perishes. All living things and the universe that were originally immortal God(Buddha) was the existence of the light of the Trinity. At that moment the Trinity was occupied by the soul of death, Satan, Satan had snatched its light, made Adam God into male and Eve God female, and they have perished in their descendant's bodies now.

However, God found out the factors that kill the children of God and has developed secretly the Sweet Dew, dreadful weapons for 6000 years, ; the light killing the soul of death, and He came to Korea in the name of Bright Star, the symbol of lily according to Him and He revealed Himself by talking the secret of the descending of the Reincarnate Maitreya Buddha and His mother's precognitive dream. The followers of the Victory Altar recognize the Seventh Angel as the Reincarnated Maitreya Buddha and Jeongdoryeong(the Savior of Koreans) who came to the world wearing human's body and will open the new heaven by changing the mortal world into an immortal one. Like this, if people do not know the circumstance of God and the essence of humans, they never know the secret of eternal life.

(3) The factor that decays blood (life) is just desires, which is the character of Satan

The foolish custom that kills God who stays in blood is the cause of death and behaviors, also the mindset killing God who is the owner of humans' lives becomes that of death, too. The Scriptures define those mindset as three poisons (covet, anger, ignorance), desire, Satan, karma, and guilt. I will call desires which cause death and are the root of sins from now on. As the Bible also says evil desire conceives and gives birth to sins; when it is full-grown, given birth to death according to James 1:15: because of desire, people commit sins, because of sins, they die. A lot of evil minds decaying blood come from desires. Sexual desires, anger, nervousness, worries, all agonies, and delusion come from desires; because of desires, there is you and I, mine and yours. So, desires make people commit sins and decays blood. Therefore, we can conclude when people know the whereabouts of sins and the secret of removing the root of sin, they cannot die. The people of the Victory Altar have learned through the preaches of the Victor, but it is not just known to the world yet.

(4) The whereabouts of sins and its character

As the cause of death comes from desires, desire itself does not attempt desire, 'I', Self-Consciousness attempts desires. Mr. Cho Hee-Sung, the seventh angel, who killed ' I ', Self-Consciousness, revealed the reason of birth, aging, diseases, and death. People die, because their blood is decayed by attempting desires, not putting on years according to Him. And He pointed out that the cause of decaying blood is Self-consciousness, the root of sin". It seems to be easy to the listeners; however, it took a long time for the Seventh Angel, the Victor, Mr. Cho Hee-Sung, to find out the secret of karma and the whereabouts of the soul of Satan through a lot of dreadful hardships and agonies that humans cannot imagine. He found out the principle of immortality through pains and bitter strife at the risk of His life that ordinary men cannot endure. Why does Self-consciousness decay blood? Because Self-consciousness is a mass of desire, poison, and a mass of sins that devils stay at. Therefore, the Bible and the Buddhist Scriptures say, "Throw away 'I' all the time,", "You can reach nirvana when you annihilate your ego." God says Self-consciousness is the home base of the soul of death through the Bible and the Buddhist Scriptures.

Nobody speaks of the whereabouts of sins in humans' history. If people commit sins, their blood is decayed. When people know the whereabouts of sins and do not commit sins, they can go toward the way of immortality, unless they remove the mind decaying blood, they cannot go toward the way of immortality. The first ancestor of humans had 100 percent clean blood. if their blood is decayed ten percent due to some reasons, the first descendants was born with the decayed blood of ten percent. As blood itself is life, blood decaying means life dying. As the history of humans' blood is humans' history, the blood have all sins of humans including the original sins of our fist ancestor, the sin of heredity, and the sin that I commit in the present life, so the blood is as bad as it can get, humans cannot avoid death. In other words, not only a personal death but also all humans' destruction come before their eyes. Satan planned the destroying all humans that are the house of God's life 6000 years ago. At the moment Satan occupied the Trinity, He became female and male humans, so they should die. Humans lost their original Self- consciousness, the true nature of God, became the slave of Satan by the Self -consciousness of Satan becoming their controlling spirit, have been deceived by the wrong information of the mind that Satan gives, and go to death according to the Seventh Angel during His preaches.

(5) The Co-Relationship the working of blood and that of mind

People think of blood as the essential material of their bodies that just provides nutrition and oxygen. However, the blood has another factor beyond the level of material. That is, the working of blood is that of mind, the working of mind is that of blood. That is, we can see that mind and blood do not exist separately; they have the same quality simultaneously. Blood is formed by the working of mind. Mind is formed by the blood. Like this, we can see that the personality and behavior is different according to the shape of blood. Therefore, the pouch of blood is called the heart, not the pouch of blood, which implies the pouch of heart. In other words, blood, mind, and bodies cannot be separated; they are one. If people think, their blood changes as they think. If somebody thinks of one person, his/ her face resembles the person that he or she thinks of. If some couples love each other, they resemble each other gradually. It is a medical and scientific truth that bodies are changed as they think. In the case of pregnant women who bear babies that do not resemble their husbands, some scholars or religions explain the phenomenon with the doctrine of reincarnation; actually, those cases are because the pregnant women thought of other men ardently or had affairs according to genetic engineering or the principle of blood. Blood has changed every second as people think. When people think of something, blood changes as people think, the blood that has the information of the material of the thought forms cells and makes the same body's shape and quality as the people thought. This is the scientific evidence that humans' bodies have been changed as they think. Also the above saying means if mind is spirit and spirit is mind, humans' bodies are spiritual ones. As spirit itself is the bodies of humans, and spirit itself is mind and thought, the saying that blood changes as people think is very scientific and medical. And to conclude, blood and mind, mind and spirit, and blood and spirit is one energy that change simultaneously. We can find a medical factor that spirit and body is one. Consequently, the change of blood and body is the product of mind's working, blood and mind has a close relationship, as the nature of mind is determined by blood. As bodies are spiritual ones that are formed by blood, if the mind changes, blood changes, if blood is changed, bodies are changed. This is the principle of blood. Heo Yong-Man, a famous cartoonist of Korea, he explained the relationship between the impression and mind through his cartoon of physiognomy. The Seventh Angel said that the basic factor of changing blood is mind, when people receive the Sweet Dew, their minds change. Also if people keep the Law of Liberty 100 percent in their lives, they can be reborn as the Holy Spirit and accomplish immortality. I will address the Law of Liberty next.

(6) The Practicing virtues of the Law of Liberty and the Secret of killing Satan

Until now, I addressed the cause of birth, aging, diseases, and death, the root and whereabouts of sins, the principle of blood, the interaction of mind and body, and the way that all humans recover God who live happily forever through knowing the essence of humans and the philosophy of one body. Then, how can we remove 'I', Self-Consciousness, the root of desires, which is the basis of all problems? This is the key of attaining nirvana. I will tell briefly the virtues that people can practice to be from the soul of death by killing Satan(滅魔滅我＝無我境地) through destroying hitting, burning, and boiling, and also tell the secret and way of reaching nirvana.

First, I will introduce seven basic practicing virtues for being free from birth and death and the teaching of the Law of Liberty, and the doctrine of the Victory Altar. They are

① Looking at the Victor, Savior God.
② Participating in services of the Victory Altar where the Sweet Dew falls every day.
③ Beseeching ardently the Sweet Dew that is necessary to destroy karma.
④ Reciting the chant of prayer for destroying Satan.
⑤ Taking a shower every day and changing clothes
⑥ Not drinking alcohol, do not smoking, overcoming sexual desire that hurt lives seriously.
⑦ Sacrificing and volunteering with the lowering attitude, and to evangelize.

By practicing these virtues, the cultivation for destroying Satan begins. When people stand on the base of the above seven basic practicing virtues, the followers of the Victory Altar think that they are ready to keep the Law of Liberty. The secret overcoming 'I', the authority of death, is keeping the Law of Liberty. The Law of Liberty is that of being reborn as the Holy Spirit, not committing sins, making blood not rot, and leading to nirvana by destroying Satan.

3. The Philosophy of Eternal Life
1) The philosophy of Han Mom and The principle of Han NaMu

All humans are surely one body because they were not fallen from the sky; they were produced by the blood of their parents. Our bodies were formed by the blood of our parents. Like this, our parents were produced by the blood of our grandparents, our grandparents were produced by the blood of our great grandparents, dating back fiftieth generation, 100th generation, and to 500th generation, we realize all humanity was formed by the blood of God, our humans' first ancestor. Therefore, all humans have the same blood, one lineage, brothers and sisters, comparing to a tree, one tree's branches have spread to six billion.

Mr. Underwood who was a missionary of Korea told an surprising fact that Koreans have served the one and only God of ancient time. Mr. Underwood said that Koreans have believed God as the one and only God. He decided to use God instead of Jehovah to do missionary work and did it actually. This philosophy of God has been connected to the thought of regarding human beings as God and has come to face the era of bearing fruit of the work of the Holy Spirit. Although the colors of skins are different due to different circumstances, looking into the skin of 1mm, all blood is red, all of them have conscience, and the character of God. Therefore, I was able to believe that all humans are one body through the same characters above. I also found that Seventh Angel told His theory logically in the aspect of genetic that all humans are surely one body and came from one root. Therefore, the Seventh Angel who was born as the Holy Spirit shouts as all humans have inherited one blood, they should regard each other as themselves. Considering that all humans' ancestors is God that is the essence of immortal life, humanity is a living thing that has come down to the present through blood, all humanity are brothers and sisters and one tree that received the same blood. Therefore, as they have been connected by one blood, the Seventh Angel shouted people to regard everybody as one body. In spite of this they are separated from brother and sister. They are one body coming from one tree and one root of one ancestor, a wrong thought that each person regards as others occupies people's minds. It is very pitiable. People should realize that this splitting mind is the soul of Satan that causes desires, occurs disputes, and insists Self-consciousness.

2) The End of History and Hananimism by The 5th waves
(1) The End of History and the Last Man

「The End of History and the Last Man」, a book written by Francis Fukuyma, an American of the second generation of Japanese who was born in Chicago had been the best-seller selected by the Washington Post consecutively for eight weeks and it had become a topic. The view on the history by Fukuyama, which is appeared in this book, is described that there is a great goal in the history of mankind and now the course of it has arrived at the terminal point. Because this great goal has been achieved since the ideology called the free democracy has been settled down throughout the world as the most idealistic form of the government.

"Our people said: The Koreans understand the word

<Hananim>; they worship him already; we have only to teach them that he is the one and only God, to tell them that his attributes are, and it will all be easy.

The Koreans also liked the idea; they knew about their old God, Hananim; it was easy for them to understand that he must receive supreme worship, and that all other gods must be ignored. This was the easy solution of the problem, and apparently it has worked well, but in my judgment it is not strictly in accorded with scriptural precept or example. 'The gods of the heathen are idols, but Jehovah made the heavens.'... A name other than His own seems almost an insult to Jehovah...

For a while, he had some Bibles, hymn-books and tracts published with the term 'Hananim' left out and another substituted, but it became increasingly hard to have this done; indeed it began to seem impossible to persist in his view if he were to remain in the mission. Afterward, light came, and he saw that he had been laboring under an error. In delving into books on Chinese and early Korean religions, he found that, at a time when only one god was worshiped in the Kingdom of Kokurei(part of early Korea), that god was called Hananim: the word was a descriptive term, signifying the great and only One.

This was different from anything he had hitherto discovered as to the Korean understanding of their use of word 'Hananim'; but as it was unquestionably the original meaning of the word, from which they had drifted away, Dr. Underwood concluded it might be used with propriety with this meaning-that its original sense might be easily recalled to the minds of the Koreans. In the light of these discoveries he felt it was entirely consistent to readily because he found there were serious difficulties attending the use of every word yet proposed." Fascism, Totalism and the Communism can no longer compete against the Free Democracy as an alternative. The history is ended now as the history of evolution of thought. Practically the end of history has come near in some countries (America, West European Countries and Japan). It is written in this book that the people living at the last stage of the history (according to the expression by Nietzsche, the last man) are wondering to seek out the meaning of life where would be no more goods to wish to acquire and things to get through fighting. Meantime, the arguments for and against Fukuyama were tremendous as much as this book had called forth a great topic. Here we would like to look upon this book from the angle through which Fukuyama established his view of history.

(2) The Society where no Egoistic men Exist

First, many readers sympathized with the point that Fukuyama considered the present time as the terminal of history. However, there are some problems for his view that the last form of the government for human being is the free democracy at present. So far development of human society has been achieved from farm and agricultural civilization of tribe community through the primitive ages to the socialism and the free democracy at present through such periods as rule by kings, aristocracy and system of theocracy. If this free democracy would be the last form of government for human being and the people who live in it would be the "last men" who lost all the desires even though they dwell in the height of prosperity and peace, there would remain not an inch of hope for mankind. Therefore, Fukuyama himself said a pessimistic word. I am also nothing but a 'bourgeois' who has various characters of the last man. I have been asking myself whether I should have been in a prison of desire for consumption or been ready to devote myself for the greatest justice and righteous things. After all, it would not so be proud to become the last man, he confessed. The communists proudly declared by utilizing the dialectic of Hegel that the capitalism would indispensably reach at the communism due to its own contradiction. And it said that form of a government. However, even though communism has been demolished already and the world of the free democracy remains unchanged yet, the latter can't be said the last form of a government, either. The end of the society in full of the egoistic people who live only for individual easiness and pleasure shall be vivid, that is to say, finally be ruined itself.

Thus, we should declare the end of history and at the same time create the new history. The entirely new man should be born next to the last man. The form of the coming society should be Hananim and the form of politics shall be rule of theocracy. The people who would live in the society shall become the new men form whom all the defects of the last man are eliminated.

(3) Hananimism and creation of the new human being

The ideology of 'Hananimism' and creation of the new human being shall be achieved in Korea just now. Because in the Bible, the Buddhist scriptures and 「Gyeokamyourok」, a Korean old book, have predicted the same.

The frame of 'Hananimism is that since all men were originally Hana(the big one), Han Namu(one tree), Han Mom Han Pi(one blood and one body) not separated genealogically as like above figures. We have to return to Hana(nim), the original shape. The mind of separating me from you should be completely eliminated and the man who becomes the state of Hana(one) shall be the new human being, the God.

Therefore, this new human being is the one who eliminated all the egoism and desires that present man keeps, in other world, eliminated the attributes of man. The man is called the God of new real human being reborn spiritually. I named them Neo-humans in this paper. The advent of the new man shall create the new age. In the new age to come in the future no man would remain alive unless he would be reborn as the God by taking off attribute of man entirely. And the new man shall never be captured by the desire of consumption as Fukuyama has worried about but be the one who devoted himself only for the greatest justice and righteous things for all of mankind. Therefore, it would be our greatest glory to be reborn as the new man though it would not be proud to become the last man.

The Last man who has built the SeungNi JeDan(Victory Altar) in Yokkok-1Dong, Buchon City, Kyeonggi-Do, South Korea and created the new human being, the God, is the very first 'New Man' for mankind. He is the very man who shall keep the pulse of history of mankind that might be cut at the time whether the history of mankind would be entirely concluded or the new history would begin.

This is the reason why the scenarios of the end of the world predicted so far by members of eschatologists have not been matched. History is proved by time. It would not take so much time until all of the people come to realize that how Mr. Hee-Sung Cho, the Victor who leads the Victory Altar creates the new history and the new man. And then I think that the new world where there are neither aging nor death shall come in the future. The Holy Dew Spirit makes us confident of eternal life.

4. The View of New Afterlife and the Super-humanism of the Victory Altar

The view of the next world and the view of the super-humanism(exodus of birth and death) of the Victory Altar is that my present life is the afterlife of my ancestors; my ancestors' lives are my previous life. Therefore, if I get out of the cycle of birth, aging, diseases, and death, I cut the causation of the three lives and enjoy nirvana. Therefore, thinking of this view, it is completely different from the view of afterlife of existing religions that people go to heaven after death. However, the will and endeavor to get out of the cycle of birth and death, to enjoy nirvana, and to recover the nature of not dying Buddha(God) are a new view of the exodus of the cycle of birth and death in the new era. That is, it is another view of getting out of the cycle of birth and death not to be conscious of death, not to adapt death, and try to overcome death. I have studied the immortal philosophy that is the view of the exodus of the cycle of birth and death to find out the whereabouts of dead spirit and the way of the exodus of the cycle of birth and death. Next, I will examine the new values of the exodus of the cycle of birth and death of the Victory Altar. Through the phrase of the Bible "Humans are like tombs!", we may think how we get out of the marsh of birth and death. The phrase makes people think of aims of their life philosophically.

"Where do humans come from and where do they go?" A lot of people study to solve this problem through all their lives. Although some scholars spent their lives solving this problem, nobody suggested the answer. Neither existing religions and new religions nor philosophy gave the answer.

1) New Values and New Philosophy of Life in the Vic-

tory Altar

'My life is only once, how can I make my short life the most valuable? Everybody experiences the period of puberty when makes adolescence think of their identity and their philosophy of life. We have faced a lot of values since we were born. There are a lot of ways, split values, seeking, and objects of life before us. The young age's dream of becoming president or general is shrunk rapidly by realizing reality as they become old. Therefore, some people's aims are eating three meals a day, some people 's are studying, some do business, some become politicians, some participate in religious activities. Some spend their lives studying a maggot, others spend their lives studying in their laboratories, some spend their lives going and out prisons due to trying to steal big money. Therefore, when they distinguish themselves in some areas, they become old and come around the corner of death. People can enjoy their lives with healthy bodies. No matter how influential geniuses are, if they die, their bodies are decayed and disappear, and people cannot approach with their spirit, what is the use of their life? Therefore, the values of life do not exist to dead people. In the end, values of their lives were empty, they lived to die, as they did not have clear values, their values of life are finished meaninglessly. The life is once no matter how happy or sad people are. To dead people, their lives are ones to die, to people who have aim to live forever, their lives are happy through their whole lives for eternal lives. Therefore, if people must live their lives, living with the hope of eternal life is not only the ground breaking mind of the Victory Altar's followers but also a meaningful philosophy. Only people who have the aim of eternal lives can have the hope of life and feel valuable about life. I think the value of a person has determined their life-span and happiness.

The members of the Victory Altar have their values in realizing of eternal life with living bodies, also being reborn as the Holy Spirit, returning God, and living as immortal being are their supreme values and happiness of life.

2) The View of Birth and Death of the Victory Altar

In the Victory Altar, the aim of faith is getting out of birth and death, returning the original God, and enjoying eternal life. Therefore, they neither even think of the term of death nor use it. Therefore, those who say that my headache is so serious, that I could just die, I am so happy, that I could just die, I am so tired, that I could just die, go to hell without realizing the sayings of the Seventh Angel. People are taken to tombs without being conscious because they are caught by Satan, their controlling spirit, are deceived, hurt themselves, and walk toward death. The members of the Victory Altar never use or think of the terms related to death. Also they try not to have the mind of dying and keep the Law of Liberty. People in the area of alternative medicine and spirit science say if people talk about something, their bodies and minds recognize their saying and their bodies and minds are accomplished as their saying with helping from their spiritual power of their saying. This fact is the result of the study of the science of spirit, which is higher than advanced science.

The Victory Altar tells that people die because of the wage of death on the basis of the Bible, James 1:15 "Evil desire conceives and give birth to sin; and sin, when it is full-grown, give birth to death." Romans 6:23,"For sin pay its wage; death" 2 King14:6 "a person is put to be to death only for a crime he himself has committed." Because the Self-Consciousness that is the root of desires control people, as God, the spirit of life, is occupied by the soul of death, lose spiritually, and God of life dies. That is the reality of death. The Victory Altar does not use the insane saying "people go to heaven after death" Also they are not deluded by such an illogical saying. Then what happens to dead people?

According to the most universal common sense, people lose their consciousness when they die. Although there is much to be desired in proving whether the spirit leaves the body or not after death, as the Bible says that after death, the spirit disappears, he Victory Altar's followers believe people die when a person's energy and spirit are destroyed completely, there is nothing to be left after death. There is no difference in weight just before death and just after death; the body gets cold gradually right after death, As soon as people die, the flowing of blood stops, the temperature of the body becomes cold, it stiffens, finally blood and body are decayed, and become soil. There is nothing left any more. Only if the man exists somewhere, he/she exists painfully in his/her children who are produced by his/ her blood, he /she faces his /her afterlife in his/her children in the present world. Therefore, if people die, their lives have no meaning and their happiness and spirit finish nothing left, therefore, they should try desperately to be born as the Holy Spirit and to recover original their light by rooting out the factors to kill people. This is a different point from other new religions. The aim of all religions is receiving salvation and achieving immortality. Humans have made their religions and have believed in their own God to live forever.

Also a lot of people such as scientists and artists have made efforts to gain true happiness. However, they have not achieved it because they did not know the cause of death and they did not find fundamental solutions for death, either. If they have found the cause of death and have removed it, immortality would be already achieved. Most scriptures such as the Bible, the Buddhist books, and prophecies predicted that the aim of all religions would be accomplished by the Victor at the end of times. However, because they have different religions and interpreted their scriptures differently, there are a lot of religious conflicts and discords between them. Therefore, so far, existing religions did not find the condition of salvation and the secret of immortality. I was able to find that each religion has the hero of its scripture; almost scriptures predicted in one voice the advent of the Victor. There are common predictions if time is ripe, the hero of all religions will appear as one person with a sign. Here are the hero's sign and the authority.

(1) He can pour out the Sweet Dew.
(2) He reveals the cause of death and teaches the way of immortality to humans
(3) He announces the essence of God and Satan and their whereabouts exactly.
(4) He can control winds and clouds at His will.
(5) He unites all religions.
(6) He makes all humans peaceful and harmonious, establishes new heaven and new earth; paradise.
(7) He makes all humans be reborn as the Holy Spirit.

The Bible says, "You don't hear while you have ears and you don't see while you have eyes." Do you know why I cite these words? Nowadays you don't see the Holy Dew spirit which the Victor pours out in the Victory Altar every day, and you can't understand the secret of immortal life, the secret of overcoming Satan which the Victor teaches you every day.

First, be empty your mind completely

What is the state of God's mind? It is not a selfish mind, but a self-sacrificing mind and a selfless mind that is not a complicated worldly thought. The Bible says, "Unlike a child, you can't enter heaven." The child has no mind. That means the child has no desire, worldly or thoughts. The Savior has fought to have an empty mind in His life. In an empty mind, there cannot be ego. The empty mind is God's mind. On the other hand, complicated worldly thoughts are Satan's mind, and the very Satan's mind is the cause of man's senility and death.

Second, walk the righteous road toward the New Heaven
Eternal life must be trodden by mind, not by body. That means you must practice the Victor's new words spiritually not physically. Mankind has only to cherish God's mind. That's all you can and must do. The moment you cherish God's mind, you become God at that moment. The road to the New Heaven is so narrow that even a camel can't enter a needle. That means the son's of the Devil can't enter the new heaven, but only the sons of God can enter the heaven. Salvation means restoring into the Holy Spirit. The ways of restoring God are cherishing God's mind, and looking at God incessantly, regarding everyone as yourself, having the self-sacrificing mind and entrusting all your life and what you have to God.

Third, know the secret of cherishing God's mind.
Man's living body is the state of his mind, the mind is the body. And blood is spirit, mind is the working of blood, and mind is spirit. His life and blood are also in his living posterity. Therefore the afterlife (the next world) just comes true in this world in his descendants' blood. That means when you are reborn into the immortal body, the souls of your ancestors in your blood also live immortally. People regard everyone as others. In fact, everyone is one because the first ancestors of humanity are Adam and Eve, and they are the sons and daughters of Adam

and Eve. Humanity cannot become God unless his mind is equivalent with God's mind, though he takes part in the service of the Victory Altar every day.

Finally, the other factors for immortality should be supplementary actions just to receive the Sweet Dew every day and know what it is; the origin and essence of the Sweet Dew. In other word, 'the hidden manna' has the same meaning as 'the Sweet Dew=甘露海印'in a Korean prophetic book. Generally, those who study about Mahayana Buddhism say Korean's Buddhism is the Maitreya thought and Japan's is Amita one when they introduce the Buddhism of Korea and Japan. We can see that these viewpoints depend on where they focus on between practice and studying of scriptures that are the core factors of Buddhism. Considering the result of studying of the Buddhist Scriptures about Buddhism, Japan's Buddhism is advanced higher than Korea. However it seems like that Korean Buddhism excels much more in practicing and Zen meditation. Actually, the studying of scriptures and cultivating should be paralleled together. If the balance is broken, it causes difficulties in realizing the truth. The reason we study scriptures is because if we do not understand exactly the key points of the prophets and the sayings of heaven, it seems like we go somewhere in the dark without lamps.

The core term that most scriptures commonly foretold is the Sweet Dew and the Holy Dew Spirit. No matter how much people read Scriptures, unless they realize the hidden truth; it is difficult to find the way to lead to nirvana. Without knowing about the original meaning of the Sweet Dew(甘露)exactly in the scriptures, nobody can reach nirvana according to Buddhist Scriptures. Also the Bible says that the man who pours down the Holy Dew Spirit is the Victor and Savior. Additionally, Revelation 2:17 records "To him who overcomes, I will give some hidden manna. I will also give him a white stone with a new name written on it, no one knows except the one who receives it." Here, 'the hidden manna' has the same meaning as 'the Sweet Dew=甘露海印' in a Korean prophetic book, 『Gyeokamyourok』. Then I will check the paragraphs about the Sweet Dew in the Bible as following.

①According to Hosea 14:5, "I (God) will be like dew to Israel(the Victor), he will blossom like lilies." God predicted that He will become Dew to the Victor and fall down.
②Isaiah 26:19 "As the sparkling dew refreshes the earth, so the Lord will revive those who have long been dead." God predicted in the Bible if the Holy Dew Spirit falls down, death will disappear on the earth exactly.
③Joel 2:28-30 "Afterwards, I will pour out my spirit on everyone: there will be bloodshed, fire, and clouds of smoke." Therefore, here, the terms of bloodshed, fire, and clouds of smoke correspond with fire=火, rain=雨, Dew=露, three abundant God's Spirit(三豊海印) in 『Gyeokamyourok』 in both eastern and western.
④Micah 5:7 "The people of Israel who survive will be like refreshing Dew sent by the Lord" The Lord says that He will send Dew to people, which means that He will attend to people as Dew like fire(火), rain(雨), Dew(露).
⑤Psalms 133:3, "It is like the dew on mountain of the Hermon, falling on the hills of Zion. That is where the Lord has promised his blessing, life that never ends." Therefore, summarizing the above sentences, I can conclude when the Sweet Dew falls down, death will disappear on the earth, and immortality is accomplished step by step. Like this, the hidden manna descending in the Victory Altar means just same as the Sweet Dew '甘露 海印' of

『Gyeokamyourok』. Almost all scriptures of the world predicted that hidden manna would fall down from heaven. If it is surely the food of gods that is predicted in scriptures, the theory of the Victory Altar that immortality with a physical body is accomplished is supported by the prediction of several scriptures and old books. Also the man who pours down the Sweet Dew and received a white stone(白石) says the name on the white stone. According to Revelation, the prophet like Moses, the Victor, and the true Savior(the Seventh Angel) is a new theory on the basis of the prediction of the Bible. Therefore, I have tried to study the hidden manna of heaven broadly and to reveal it clearly for a long time. When, in old China, when emperors governed the country benevolently(仁政), they thought the Sweet Dew would come down from heaven as a sign for a happy occasion. That is, it is sweet immortal medicine. In Korea, there is a saying that sin son (神仙), who is beyond the level of human eat the Sweet Dew. Also Koreans enjoy the Sweet alcohol(甘酒), the traditional beverage. Scholars do not know well whether the origin of the Sweet Dew came from China or India. When it is interpreted as 甘露 in Buddhist scriptures, I am sure that Sanskrit's 'amrta' was interpreted amita(阿彌陀)in Chinese letter. In my opinion, the origin of the word for the Sweet Dew spread to each country through Buddhist sutra of ancient India when the culture of Eastern and Western was intersected. I think that 『Greek mythology』, 『Sanhaegyeong=山海經』, a prophetic of China, and 『Gyeokamyourok』, a Korean prophetic book are the key to interpreting the origin of the word. Then I will examine Amrta in ancient myths and literatures. Amrta has the same origin as ambrosia in 『Greek mythology』, which is a beverage for the gods, if people drink it, they neither grow old nor die. Originally, it means 'to pour the power of life'. According to linguists, it is interpreted as a(without=無)+mrta(death=死) by

Indians. That is, it means immortality「不死」by prefix 'a(無 without)' going in front of 'mrta(死 death)'. The more interesting thing is that word of 'ambrosia' is being analyzed in the same way as amrta. The analyzing of the origin of ambrosia is that ambrosia<ambrotos=immortal(a=not +brotos=mortal). Also, the Sweet Dew is quoted frequently as the synonym of nirvana. When people call Buddhism 'the Dharma-door of the Sweet Dew=(甘露의 法門)', in this case, they regard nirvana as the accomplishing of immortality by the Sweet Dew. Therefore, they think that the basic aim of Buddhism is reaching nirvana by receiving the Sweet Dew. According to the '普門品' of the Lotus Sutra(法華經), the Sweet Dew removes any agony from birth, aging, disease, death of humans due to worldly desires. That is, the hidden manna, the Holy Dew Spirit, and the Sweet Dew are the core terms of all scriptures to give immortality. In other words, the terms indicate the Spirit of the Victor, the Maitreya Buddha, appears to the world to save humanity at the end of times. Surprisingly, the predictions of all scriptures have been accomplished 100 percent in the Victory Altar as they foretold.

CHAPTER V
The New Reseach Method of NRMs & New Public Philosophy

1. The New Method of New Religion Research

1) The task and aim of the study is seeking whereabouts of the dead spirit and the method of exodus from birth and death

How do humans like spiritual tombs get out of the pain of birth and death? Where do humans come from, where do humans go? A lot of people have spent their lives addressing this question; however, so far, nobody has suggested a clear answer. Also, the philosophies of religions did not give the answer. All religions have the view of soul and spirit(靈魂觀), which is when people die, their spirit leaves the body and goes to the world where only spirits gather. The belief in the separation of spirit and body(靈肉分離) and the view of the afterlife (來世說) based on the belief have always been the foundation of religions. After people die, the temperature of their bodies starts getting cold, the circulation of the blood stops, and the bodies stiffens. Finally the blood rots, the flesh rots, bones rots and become soil. Like this, do people have to die in the era when the Sweet Dew falls down, too? The exodus from the cycle of birth and death is the ultimate aim of all religions and the task of study in the history of humans so far. Also my aims of studying new religions are studying of the exodus from the cycle of birth and death that has been cherished-desire of humans and seeking the methodology of exodus from the cycle of birth and death.

2) The Motive of Study

I enjoyed books on religion. However there were neither true and immortal(不死) religion nor the right way(正道). Therefore, I did not have any religion. That is because my mother advised me to have the right view of religions at an early age. She said that people go to churches or temple to pray for a little hope and worldly desires without washing their mind, emptying their mind, and living as their conscience, you don't have to have religions that tell people to go heaven or the land of happiness by believing someone, although you do not go to churches or temples, it is okay if you neither have shames to God nor deceive your conscience. My mother became a widow at age 29. However, she took the role of my father and teacher and taught life to me correctly. As well, I did not value at studying religions because religions did not say the secret of exodus of birth and death.

People have thought that the basic aim and value of religion is eternal life with living bodies, prophets predicted that such paradise would be built in Korea through books. However, so far immortal nonpolar Great-Dao(大道)has not existed in the world. Longing for the hope of eternal life and realizing nonpolar great Dao(無極大道) are a foremost goal to me and scholars who have studied Scriptures or who received the duty of heaven. Therefore, the starting of studying religion is a rational and reasonable thought. The approaching method is right in studying Scriptures, and it is natural attitude to those who seek the right way and research religions.

As I have not found the religion that accomplishes eternal life and insists the Right-Dao(正道), the convincing propagation of college students of the Victory Altar made me confirm the religion twenty years ago in Donga University. The studying of the new philosophy of eternal life of the Victory Altar through participating observation and experience started at that time. During the period of twenty-one day education, people see what the Victory Altar is. It is impossible to learn the methodology and a lot of information in a short time that a lot of seers and prophets have studied. Therefore, unless they try intensively to learn the principle of immortality, it is impossible to understand it. Additionally, unless the researcher studies in a long view and experiences the principle, to write a thesis about new immortal science is a reckless challenge as a conscientious scholar. Therefore, to maximize the outcome of the study, I became a member of the followers who pursuit eternal life.

3) The Methodology that is attempted for the first time and the process of the study

Above I said when a researcher studies a religion; the quality and the result of the study are determined by whether the researcher becomes a member of the religion or not-. Unless the researcher becomes one with the members of a religion which he studies, it becomes a thesis written by a researcher remaining a mere spectator. Like Dr. Kim Jong-Seok said in his thesis about neo-humans in 2009, there are a lot of methodologies in studying new religions; we can find considerable problems in the methodologies. By what aim the researcher has and what special intentions the researcher has, the truth of religions might be distorted. When a researcher studies with a negative view, the result of the studying has no results, unknowing its taste. Without analyzing their spiritual changing, they arrange contents which are going around existing materials, and draw conclusions of the thesis at the level of his subjective and religious knowledge. Therefore, I chose the methodology of participant observing and practicing like the members of the

Victory Altar to know their thought and the phenomenon of their spirit not to make mistakes in my analysis. Also, I have studied focusing on all the followers becoming one by researching not only Scriptures provided by each religion but also new Scriptures from Confucianism, Buddhism, and Christianity including all Scriptures existing around the world. It's better expression that I chose Trinity methodology in studying the truth of eternal life.

First, understanding through the way of participant observing
Second, the choice of methodology of analyzing the doctrine and the real phenomenon through participant observing there.
Third, the introduction of a new methodology of studying researcher's body and mind by a methodology of observing self through practice and experiment.

So far, there are few researchers who studied through the third methodology of participating and practicing. This new Methodology of Field Study(臨地研修)which a researcher goes to local site, looks at, listens to, gets information, and writes theses is used in Japan when scholars of religions and cultural anthropology study. I think using this methodology is suitable for me to study the new special phenomenon of the Victory Altar which speaks of the first immortal nonpolar Dao(無極大道) in human history'. When a researcher study the medical world, physics, or religious science uses the methodology of participant observing, and the researcher speaks of them subjectively or writes his thesis without experiencing some parts, he/she distorts the facts. The contents of the thesis are different from the reality. Tak, M H of researchers of religions researched the Victory Altar without participating, thinking about its contents through his subjective thought, and threatening by demanding money to the religion.

This thesis is a part of theses I have studied for twenty years. I arranged only the religious phenomenon of the Victory Altar, a new religion of Korea, and the philosophy of immortality under the subject "The Exodus out of birth and death", which if people's bodies change by receiving the Sweet Dew, they can accomplish immortality. I did it to help researchers about the Victory Altar and outsiders of it to know easily. There was a lot of persecution from the government, broadcastings and newspapers, and mass media by announcing distorted information. Therefore, I was able to see that the image of the Victory Altar has been damaged for thirty years. Also, I will reveal that the mass media distorted in reporting about the Victory Altar missing the Reincarnate Maitreya Buddha's working with His other selves, His amazing accomplishments of the Five Covenants, mysterious spiritual experiences, and falling the Sweet Dew that are very beneficial to all humans. The Victory Altar has been persecuted most among new religions of Korea by other religions and mass media and is recognized as an illegal unreasonable religion in Korea. Therefore, it should be corrected immediately in the view of world religious cultural history.

Furthermore, the Seventh Angel was persecuted more severely than the man who talked about the Copernican System for talking about eternal life with living bodies in public for the first time in humans' history though all humans die. According to my long research, there has been a big difference between the facts about the Victory Altar and information that were reported perversely to the society of Korea. There are a lot of proofs, the pictures of the Sweet Dew, the materials about the Sweet Dew in Scriptures that researchers can collect in the Victory Altar. I want to say that the religious phenomenon of the Victory Altar, peculiarity, and identity should be understood not discriminated or criticized.

My aim of participant observation is to confirm that the immortal science of the Seventh Angel is reasonable and logical in the aspects of Scriptures, medical science, and spiritual science. If the immortal science of the Victory Altar is accomplished as He says and it is verified truly, it will be great accomplishment in religious history, a ground breaking spiritual changing, and the revolution of science and revolution. As now is the time to suggest the practicing methodology, with it, I can share the immortal science with all humans. I arranged the thesis of the immortal principle using a new method, the method of self-practice and experiment observation', through practicing. Also high spiritual phenomenon that cannot be expressed or explained in human language becomes my object of study. Therefore there are a lot of mysterious materials in the result of the study, enough to make scholars of new religions and the members of the academy surprised. I will introduce the result of the study in detail through self-practice and experiment in the seminar of 'Neo-Humans research' and in journal of the International Academy of Neo-Humans Culture', Now I will introduce only the outline of the core study in this thesis. I have studied the phenomenon of physical and spiritual changing objectively as possible as I could. I used the terms used in the Victory Altar neither to cling to the terms of social knowledge nor to distort its character, but because there were neither theses nor theories, it is impossible to explain a lot of facts in the Victory Altar using the existing terms. Therefore, I think when new theories are introduced, as there were no previous examples, researchers do not have to use the trite terms of existing religions. Also, the principle of the Victory Altar should be evaluated with conscience. There are a lot of bulipmunja(不立文字

=meaning that cannot express with letters), bulyeon(不然=not so), or giyeon(其然=meaning something is correct in the view of God, but it seems like to be not correct on the view of humans=不然). For example, eternal life is accomplished surely in the view of God. However it is not accomplished in the view of humans. I recommend that people read the sayings and theory of immortality with spirit. Also, as it is neither a worldly common principle nor a worldly doctrine, that should not be judged by humans' common sense. In addition, I hope this thesis will be helpful for scholars of non-followers of the Victory Altar and the believers of other religions to understand the Victory Altar easily. Then I will examine the view of afterlife and the view of the exodus of birth and death of the Victory that corresponds to the current of the world and this era.

2. What is the Han-moum Philosophy?

Today's humanity and the earth are influenced a lot by the changing process of the solar system and galaxy, including the principle of the change of the universe. However, the environmental problems, the food problems, and the conflict and hostility between religions bring about more critical situation to humanity. In such situation, humanity needs new bright wisdom and a philosophy of life to accomplish true happiness and peace. In this respect, I will suggest 'The Philosophy of Han-moum', be a new alternative philosophy to bring peace and hope to humanity, which will recover human being, and become a philosophy to save humanity's life.

First, I will point out the current address and their roles of modern philosophies. I will also diagnose and discuss the limit and problems of modern philosophies.

In the body, I will introduce 'The Philosophy of Han-moum'

that appeared as an alternative that will be the way to become a true peace to humanity and save humanity's life. Moreover, I will speak about a new philosophy of eternal life that is based on 'The Philosophy of Han-moum', that is occurring in Korea.. Further, I will explain about the result of studying Korean new religions for 20 years on the basis of new eternal life of neohumans.

Lastly, I will examine whether there are not problems in the research methodology of modern philosophies and selecting the object of research. Also I will search the direction that modern philosophy should go, the way of humanity's true happiness and peace. I am sure that people will realize that 'the Hanmoum Philosophy' has a philosophical clue, which humanity get out of his ego that is a spiritual prison to restrain humanity. People will realize through my paper the essence of Utopia and Ego that they have never experienced before, the Western philosophers will be fresh shocked by the heaven of neohumans' heart of the East. In this respect, my thesis has an important meaning.

Additionally, they will build the Visible Idea world in their bodies. Also those who understand the way of removing Ego will become Neo-humans and will become perfect God that does not die.

1) Where is the present state of the modern philosophies?

Some astronomies and physicists of the universe insist that zero points or turning point is coming soon; that is, 'Photon Belt', the era of the photon, is impending. However, the old books and prophecies tell about a lot of messages to survive in the new era to humanity, who is facing this change in the environment of the earth, and the big change of the cosmos. The predictions said the advent of the New Philosophy of Immortality, the new life that Neo -humanities are aiming, foretold the finishing of the life of worldly desire coming from the material civilization, and the era of light that needs the revolution of consciousness of humanity.

2) I participated in the XXII World Congress of Philosophy in Seoul.

Where around 2600 famous philosophers gathered there. The title of the congress was 'Rethinking Philosophy Today'. I remember the title clearly because the congress told me that so far there were no true philosophies or thought, and made me rethink the definition of philosophy and its role. So I will go to Athens to join the congress. God predicted the future in the Bible and the Buddhist books. The Bible said that religions and philosophies which have sought the truth and the Idea World without knowing the essence of God and humanity are not perfect and the expediential sayings of the Bible are not perfect, either. So in Corinthian 13:8-10 "8. Charity never fails: but whether there be prophecies, they shall fail; whether there be tongues, they shall cease; whether there be knowledge, it shall vanish away." , "9. For we know in part, and we prophesy in part.", "10. But when that which is perfect is come, then that which is in part shall be done away."

While studying the prophecies of the world for 20 years, I found it is the time the Bible predicted, because I have collected its evidences and signs a lot. The Bible predicted that a new philosophy would appear, its aim is that God makes people believe the new era will come. So John 14 : 29 said, "And now I have told you before it come to pass, that, when it is come to pass, ye might believe. "Additionally, John 16 : 13 said, "Howbeit when he, the Spirit of truth, is come, he will guide you into all truth:

for he shall not speak of himself; but whatsoever he shall hear, that shall he speak: and he will show you things to come." The above words predicted that in the era of change, the Holy Spirit would come, pour His Spirit, and lead people to the way of truth, and say what would happen in the future. Also the Bible said, "If the Spirit of the truth comes, He will teach the perfection, pour the grace of wisdom and the Holy Spirit to the children of light first to make them see God face to face." 1 Corinthians 13:12 predicted, "For now we see through a glass, darkly; but then face to face: now I know in part; but then shall I know even as also I am known."

Philosophy should study and suggest the methodology to solve the complicated problems of not only the global village but also humanity, such as where do the conflict of humanity come from?, 'What is humanity? 'What is the root of humanity?', 'How should humanity live?', 'Who am I?' and so on.

So far, the present state of the modern philosophies has stuck to only an ideological theory that comes from the ignorant spirit of death. What is true peace and true happiness? The absences of the realistic philosophy which can lead people in wandering and crisis. There have been a lot of philosophers and religionists including Socrates, but nobody did not complete philosophies which can suggest the certain answers to the problems of long-cherished wish of humanity and salvation. I think that the aim of the Idea World is in realizing everlasting happiness and the philosophy of immortal life. Due to this periodical necessity, I will announce the philosophy of immortality. Also I will introduce a new philosophy to the philosophical world, which is the 'the Hanmoum Philosophy' based on 'the theory of one tree', which is the practical methodology to support in accomplishing the philosophy of immortality, so I will put it as the subtitle of title of my thesis. Those who remove their Ego and fixed idea can see the secret of immortal life in the body. By practicing it, they will feel the essence of the Holy Spirit and new heaven in their bodies and mind by God in their bodies defeating Ego.

Now, by the advent of the Victor of the east, the great philosopher, who overcame the spirit of ignorance, Ego, all philosophers can realize in their mind the Idea World which philosophers have sought so far. It is the time when people can feel the Original True Nature of God in their bodies. Additionally, by campaigning all humanity to become one, this thesis will be the alternative to overcoming the crisis of humanity and the earth which is at stake. Also, this thesis will give new hope to humanity who has wandered by the philosophies and value which came from the spirit of death so far. I hope that the thesis will be the starting point which people get out of the thought of philosophers and religion which are wandering in all kinds of superstitions and delusions.

3) What is the limit of the present philosophies?

So far, the limit of philosophies is that they could not suggest the answer to the questions, 'Who am I?', and 'What is the essence of humanity?' Philosophers did not give answers to even these two questions. Some anthropologists, scientists, and religionists believe in the old evolution theory, that humanity evolved from amoeba or monkeys. Theologians, who believe in God, believe the doctrine of creation that humanity was created by God, have the view of afterlife that people go to heaven after death. I am sure that their thought, elusions, philosophies will collapse by the philosopher of immortality.

If there are philosophers who realize the limit of all philosophers, they will be ready to experience the philosopher of new life and the Visible Idea World. Immanuel Kant who insisted to put together the experientialism and rationalism in 18th century spoke of "there exists a philosophy where people realize precisely the limit of philosophies." Kant predicted 200 years ago that the philosopher who knows the limit of philosophers would appear. Genius single Kant insisted that humanity gain knowledge from experiences and rations. He called 'the phenomenon world' which people can see. He called 'Transcendental' the world of life as it is, that is, the essence of inner, all 'the world of foreknowledge' called the world of immaterial unseen like elementary particle, so which people cannot feel with their six senses. Especially, considering from the history and development of the western philosophy, it started from natural philosophy through the ration of humanity, passing through rationalism and experientialism, and social utilitarianism and pragmatism led and governed the West of 18th and 19th century. The doctrine of creation and the theory of evolution which Democracy supports become the limit of philosophy, materialism coming from the contradiction of communism, the dichotomous way of thinking of coming from the theory of relativity, the spread of individualism have become harmful factors to the society. Furthermore, philosophy did not give the answers to the basic questions 'What is the essence and the original nature of humanity?', 'What is righteousness? 'What is the common goodness of humanity?' Socrates who is the founder of ethical philosophy said, "Know yourself." However, modern philosophers did not know precisely even the true Ego of humanity. That is the current state of today's philosophy.

In spite that so far philosophies did not tell even the pseudo Ego from true Ego, was there the philosophy? That is the question that I want to ask to the philosophers. Through this philosophy congress, philosophers will know the limit of modern philosophy clearly.

4) The problems in the subjects of study of philosophy and the methodology

People usually think the birthplace of philosophy is Greece. However Western philosophy did not research philosophically about the essence and life of humanity, the subject of philosophy and did not have a practical philosophy, either. Also although the subject of philosophy is humanity, the methodology based on natural science and material and researched with their wrong ration of humanity undergoing trial and error with repeat, so nobody experiences the Idea world. Some scholars think the starting of Eastern philosophy was late. In fact philosophy of the east started quietly early. While studying the history and books of old Korean, I could see that Eastern philosophy of the east started quietly early from religion such as harvest ceremonies and the thought of humanity being God, the faith of Maitreya, thought of hoped for the Messiah, so there are a lot of the record of their study of philosophy.

The feature of Eastern philosophy is that it started from the root and nature of humanity and nature to the aim and its role of philosophy. For example, the study of 'what is the root of humanity?', 'the study of philosophy and the value of humanity about ethics' 'The essence and wisdom of God' came from ancient time. Of course, there were such studies in the West, but the subject of the study of philosophy and the methodology were wrong. So nobody could talk about the philosophy of the truth. The philosophy of the true can talk about the essence of sin and humanity, the secret of eternal life easily and reasonably. For these reasons, it is natural that a great philosopher who gives the hope of the future to humanity comes from the East. A lot of prophets of the world including Tagore of India and prophetic books foretold in one voice that a perfect philosophy that save all humanity of the world will come from Korea that will be the light of the East. To conclude, the endeavor to find new heaven and the Idea world not exterior material world or ideological cosmos but in the mind of humanity was progressed from the ancient time. Examining the history of the philosophy of ancient Korea from faith and the philosophy of religion, its philosophy focused on wakening the nature of humanity and recovering his original mind. Regardless of the East and the West, so far people failed in finding the wisdom of light because their consciousness were caught by ignorance and delusion. I think there are three kinds of methodology of philosophy and religion in order for the study of philosophy to be effective.

First is the methodology of a theoretical approach which researchers collect material by following books and the recording of theses about philosophy in the history of philosophy and religion.

Second is participant observation which researchers participate in the real activity of religions by using material and information already collected. Usually most philosophers and religious researchers use these methodologies and conclude.

Therefore, I don't like their methodology because they are not enough to be clear theses. I think the best methodology is that the subject of study and observer should be studied at the same time in the neutral and objective situation on the basis collected material. Furthermore, on the methodology I adopt a unique method, self-experimental practice method, for 20 years, to study phenomenon of new religion and philosophy. I talked with the followers of the religions about their philosophy and studied using my mind and body as a laboratory on the basis of consistency of speech and the theory and the words. And through hands-on experience and the methodology of learning the result through self-experiment, I checked and diagnosed the two theories and the factors of real phenomenon, wrote a thesis by the data of the result of the study. I think there were few philosophers in the history of philosophy who wrote theses through studying philosophy using this methodology for 20 years. I adopt a new methodology in this thesis, too. I will mention about the terms of methodology about the philosophy of immortality in the conclusion.

5) The Philosophy of Immortality & (Han-moum Philosophy)

What is the philosophy of immortality which appeared by periodical necessity and will accomplish new heaven. The original title of my thesis is that of Korean style, I drafted 'Han-moum Philosophy though Han-pi Principle'. However in order for Western philosophers to easily understand my thesis, I changed its title into 'the Philosophy of Immortality & Visible Idea World' (Focused on the Holistic Ontology by One Tree Theory). Everybody has a different value of life and a different way of life in accordance with his philosophy. The thinking way and action of humanity, character building, the shape of humanity are different in accordance with which value people have. Additionally, by what aims people have and where they put their meaning of life, the voyage of life is changed, the happiness and satisfaction of life is changed. In this respect, the philosophy and value of life and the aim of life are very important. So far, because humanity has wrong values and philosophy, conflicts and wars due to the misunderstanding from communication, and wrong desires, he becomes the slave of the spirit of ignorance, wander in agonies and pains, and die without living less 100 years. Now to humanity who is welcoming the era of the light of new heaven, the true so far hidden by darkness and ignorance has been revealed gradually. The Idea world which countless philosophers and prophets have only dreamed of is coming into view. The philosophy of immortality about new heaven appeared with the campaigning of saving life by making the world peaceful, and all humanity as one. I will introduce it as a new philosophy. The true study and true philosophies should be so simple, clear, and universal that everyone can learn and practice it easily. Then I will explain the philosophy of immortality and the Han-moum Philosophy from the point of view of Holistic Ontology using the Principle of Hanna-mu and the principle of one blood. What is the Philosophy of Immortality?

In short, so far, humanity has put philosophical value on thought, religion, and philosophy which were born under the death, the world of material to decay and perish. However, the philosophy of immortality studies the secrets to overcoming death and killing Ego, the way to become immortal one with being alive, and return to immortal God by practice the new immortal study in everyday life. That is, the philosophy of immortality can be understood easily through the glossography of 'Han' and 'Han-moum', and 'Han-namu'. Also I will explain the philosophy of immortality figuratively using one tree and the principle of one blood.

The principle of Han moum is that all humanity on the earth are the offspring of God, the first ancestor, comparing to a tree, like 7 billion 's branch of one big tree, all humanity is Han moum. Using a philosophical term, the principle of Han moum is included 'Focused on the Holistic Ontology', which has the meaning 'many is one', the meaning of Holistic One is that small many one is in Big One, paradoxically, on the contrary, essentially, men and women, old men and young men have different color of skin, the root is one. String theory is the same principle as the philosophy of Hanmoum. The body and mind of humanity is like a organically connected tree; they received one blood and are a tree of life with 7 billion people. This new philosophical term expresses a corporate body of Han, a noun of Hana meaning a big organic mass, and body. This philosophical terms are seen in the Korean traditional thought, 'Hananim(The God of Lord)Thought', which Koreans believed the one and only God, it is an expression of heaven coming down from ancient Korea. 'Han' of 'Han Thought' has a profound philosophical meaning. 'Han' has a meaning not only 'One' but also more than 20 other meanings, it is an ancient philosophical Korean which is related heaven and God. Now I will examine the philosophical meaning of 'Han'. A lot of new meanings have been added to the early definitions of the word 'Han'. According to Ahn Ho-Sang the current definitions of 'Han' are as follows: 1) great; 2) east; 3) bright; 4) oneness; 5) unification; 6) people; 7) old; 8) wholeness; 9) beginning; 10) Han people; 11) white; 12) light; 13) high; 14) same(ness); 15) many(ness); 16) sky or heaven; 17) long; 18) great leader; 19) up; 20) king; 21) perfect; and 22) inclusiveness. And 'Han' use as noun, adjective, adverb, suffix and prefix, can be attached to various words to indicate the above implications. My special research fall upon the six most general and popular dictionary meanings. According to the Korean-English Dictionary, the word 'Han' implies six different meanings as follows: 1. hana(하나, meaning, one: e.g. han-hae(한 해, meaning, a year)); 2. gattun(같은, meaning, the same: e.g. han-jipe(한집에 (in the same house)); 3. o-n(온-, meaning, whole: e.g. o-n gyuul(온-겨울 throughout(all) the winter)); 4. han-chang(한창, meaning(the peak: e.g. han-gyuul, (midwinter))); 5. han-gaunde(한가운데, meaning(the middle: e.g. han-bam(midnight))); 6. Yak(약, meaning, approximately: e.g. han-sipbun(about ten minutes)). Being holistic in one's thinking is also to be both horizontal and vertical, both subjective and objective. Therefore thinking of Holistic Ontology can often be Paradoxical as well, for in such holistic thinking One is Many and Many are One. In holistically inclusive or holistic otology thinking the subject is the object, and vice versa. In this intrinsically circular, harmonious and symbiotic way of thinking, woman is man, and man is woman. They are of course different from each other. But they are fundamentally the same blood and equal body as humans who come from the original God. This holistic ontology way of thinking is the most fundamental and characteristic aspect of the Korean way of thinking. Also this like the 'Han', 'Hanna-nim Thought', 'Hanism', 'Hannaism', 'Han-jibung Han-gazok', 'Han-minzok', 'Han-gyere', 'Han-hyeangje(one brother), 'Han-moum(unit one body)', 'Han-maum(same one mind)', 'Han-namu(same one tree) w/holism is endlessly broad, deep, and organic inclusive. They have both physical and metaphysical (i.e. spiritual and optical) dimensions in them. I could see that all humanity is one brothers, one family, one body, all races are the people of God, and one tree through 'Han', 'Hananim Thought', 'One Tree Theory' in the body of this thesis supports it. According to the recording of Herbert foreign missionary, it said that Koreans believed Hana-nim, the one and only God of the beginning. The reason that Koreans have had this thought is because the possibility that they are the tribe of Dan among the lost ten tribe is very high. The phrases of the

Bible that support the Han moum philosophy are as follows; Acts17:26 said about the root of humanity's blood that "From one man he made every nation of men, that they should inhabit the whole earth; and he determined the times set for them and the exact places where they should live" And Genesis 6:4, Deuteronomy 14:1, 1John 3:2, Romans 8:14-16, Psalm 82:6, John 10:35, and Proverbs 12:23 said about the root and the starting point of humanity. By putting these things together, we can see humanity is the children of the most high, is originally God. However, people do not know the secret that humanity was God of heaven. I could see the etymologic origin of such 'Hanaism' and 'Hana-nim Thought' through studying 'Arirang' Korean Folksong Examining the etymologic origin of Arirang' Korean Folksong, I could understand why the people of the world like and are moved by Arirang, the ancient Korean folk song.

Like I mentioned above, by the one blood of ancestors, all humanity who form their bodies and live common life are divided into several billions, they are one tree which is essentially unified and has the same nature and the same conscience. Therefore, regarding everybody as one body, one brother, and my body and serving everybody as God are the Han Moum philosophy. And by practicing the Han Moum Philosophy, the body of humanity is completed as that of immortal God. That is the philosophy of immortality. So far, humanity has not regarded everybody as my body, or one body. Although humanity is one body, regarding everybody as others, are sins, the working and the philosophy from selfish and wrong self-center thought and consciousness are sins, too. The sins emit the poison of desires, lead humanity to death. The Bible predicted the root and the essence of wisdom as follows. James 1:15 pointed out the essence of desire and death. When we think where the mind that regards everyone as others with worldly desires and dichotomy thought, hate, are jealous of, fight and kill come from, and what is the original nature of humanity, humanity has lived to pursue philosophy for thousands years with being crazy, by the power of ignorant consciousness. Now when all humanity realize that they are one body, one brother, and one family, and practice the Han Moum Philosophy, the philosophy of immortality is understood and completed. 'What is the Han-moum Philosophy? How is individual who has different bodies and minds one body? A lot of people may think like that, this theory has a highly philosophical factor. First, to understand the Han-moum Philosophy, people should know the Principle of Han-namu(One Tree Theory) and the Principle of Han-pi(One Blood Theory).

Comparing the bodies and minds of humanity to the basis on the above mentioned 'Focused on the Holistic Ontology, humanity is like a big tree which has the same root and branches into 7 billion. Therefore, because the thick trunks and boughs of a tree come from one root, the essence of the tree is one root, is the form that one body spreads out. Like the principle of one tree, although humanity is divided into 7 billion of bodies, minds, and blood, the essence and character of the mind, and the essence of the blood are the same, the body of humanity has the life and the mind, the figure of humanity is similar. Because 7 billion humanity were made of one blood, though their bodies are separated, the blood, mind, spirit that work in the bodies are the almost same. Only pseudo Ego which is different from the original mind, consciousness and the original genetic trait make all people look different from each other and controls to regard everybody others. However, the original mind is God, good conscience itself. All humanity who is caught by the Ego does not know this fact. If people realize that all humanity is one body, God, the children of the most high, they can see the peace and happiness of humanity around them can become free existence from the restraint of devils, and reinstate the nature of God by receiving eternal life. 'The mind regarding everybody as my body, regarding everybody as God' is the new philosophy which accomplishes immortality, is the secret that does not commit sins, is the immortal medicine which does not decay blood, and is the mind that can become one with the spirit of Idea Form.

5) The Principle of Han-pi
(1) What is the principle of blood?
Those who have a spiritual eye feel that the philosophy of bright wisdom appeared through this thesis. This new philosophy of bright wisdom of eternal life was not on the earth so far, it was predicted in the Bible, is the light of wisdom to reveal the secret of heaven, and is the bright philosophy of wisdom by the pouring of oil of the Holy Dew Spirit. Becoming the slave of death and darkness, being caught by Ego, living and using by the direction of their pseudo master, and die. That is the result of the philosophy of empty life. Now, the Victor being called the righteous man of the east who overcame the spirit of death and broke the prison of the ignorant spirit appeared in Korea. Due to the victory of the man, the philosophy of immortality, the philosophy of victory, was completed. Therefore, my thesis is about the philosophy of salvation, a new science, the philosophy of the truth of Neo-human that after a man escaped from the consciousness of death, received the true freedom, and became a Victor, the transcendent existence.

According to a New Saying of the Victor philosopher (Cho Hee-seung) on 1987. 5. 3, and 2001. 2. 8 in the SeungRi-JeDan(Victory Altar), humans are one body because they have the same first ancestors, Adam and Eve. As they have the same ancestors, they have the same blood. Having the same blood means the same people. Adam and Eve lived in the Garden of Eden. Only God lives in the Garden of Eden. So the Bible says that where God resides, heaven is. Adam and Eve lived in the Garden of Eden in heaven. Therefore, they were Gods. And their offspring are Gods, too. Puppies are dogs, calves are cows genetically. The children of God are God, too. The evidences are that humans want to live forever in infinite happiness like God though everyone dies. The reason is that their ancestors' blood that experienced immortality flows in their offspring now. So all people, whoever they are, are Gods.

Also every individual is not separated from each other; it is spiritually as one lump of same blood from the god of Lord. Because the spirit of Adam and Eve 6000 years ago is living with as people's spirit now. Adam and Eve have been one body generation by generation. This means that the whole universe is my body primarily. Accordingly, The Victor philosopher tells people to regard others as their bodies. The reason the universe moves is because as God exists in the universe, life exists, the subject of life is God. However, advanced scientists do not know it.

And then, where does the spirit of dead people exist? As blood in their living children's bodies is their ancestors' blood, it is the spirit of their ancestors. Therefore, the spirit of ancestors is not separated from that of their offspring, but the same one. It is one body. It means the spirit of ancestors is mine, and my spirit is ancestors'. The theory of this saying is new. Therefore, the spirit of ancestors lives in their offspring after their death. The ancestors who died 6000 years ago live in the present. Accordingly, the spirit of ancestors is not separated from mine. Satan has deceived us like that we are separated from each other. Actually parents and grandparents are I. Hence, I becoming a Victor philosopher against the Ego of Satan means parents becoming the Victors, my grandparents becoming the Victors. The spirit of all ancestors in the Victor becomes the Victors in my body and blood.

This new science of 'Immortality Philosophy' is perfect science. No matter how many people are, the philosophy can make all of them God. You should become a Victor by practicing the science of the eternal life. The Victor philosopher told everyone to regard others as yours. Regard anybody's fault and sin as yours, other's pains, yours. That is the mind of God and the character of God. That is just the mind of God and the character of God. It means there is neither you nor I, but one body. And then all humans become one. Also, it gives all humans peace. Therefore, the Victor told people to regard every one as their bodies. Actually they are Han-moum(one body} and one family and one brother in this world. Accordingly, if you want to be God, you should have the mind of God like that. If you have the mind that I am separated from others, you cannot become God. You are finished as Satan' human. Therefore you should always have the mind of the Holy Spirit giving from God. The SeungRi-Jedan(Victory Altar) is the place where you cultivate to live forever. The philosophy of Han-moum(one body) of regarding everyone as mine will be the truth that saves people and gives people peace. As the Victor philosopher is trying to reunify the world to make one body, Satan is copying to reunify the world. To reunify the world, they need logic and weapons to reunify the world. Whoever is one body, has the same blood, and is all my body. As nobody is not my body, if people think that everybody regard as their bodies or one body, they cannot but unify and become one body. All of mankind will become one spiritually, no matter who they are. As they are one body, they should be unified spiritually and consciously, but actually they are not. Because Satan makes people think individually.

All humans were made of blood of one God; however, they have been divided into 7 billion's Self-Consciousness for 6000 years. Even though they are one body, they do not know it, so they make boundary, fight each other, and live selfishly. The Self-Consciousness in humans is a dividing soul; also it is the evil soul that is the factor of quarrel, confusion, anguish, unhappiness, and death. As well, it is the reason of lost paradise (Idea world), the birth and death of the universe, and miserable humans' history according to the Victor. No matter how good people are, they have Self-Consciousness, individual consciousness, and self-esteem, it is evil and dirty Satan. Now as we found the factor of death, we should go back to the original being by removing the factor of death. All humans can return one heart of the God. The Victor tells, "the truth is in one, peace is in one, and immortality is in one." After the Savior Victor appeared, the directions of all humans' fates were already decided. The Victory Altar(SeungRi-JeDan) campaigns all humans to be one. As the Savior of the Victor philosopher came, the perfect Holy Spirit of truth came like the Bible predicts in Corinthians 3. The perfect Holy Spirit of truth is just the Holy Dew Spirit according to Isaiah 26:19 and Hosea 14:5, the Spirit of the last Angel in John' prediction, and the fruit of life in Revelation. The Holy Dew Spirit is the last weapon of the Savior of Victory God for Satan that will recover the original paradise from the lost Paradise. The strong Holy Spirit that makes 7 billion humans as one is working now. The Satan which knows his fate goes into humans and makes a frantic last-ditch effort. The Satan that drives all humanity to destruction by seducing people is Self-Consciousness hiding in humanity. As Self-Consciousness is the factor of destroying humanity, overcoming Self-Consciousness is the way to achieve salvation and peace. Therefore, the Idea World and Ideal Form exist in the heart of 'Super-Ego and Superhuman'. So far, I examined the philosophy of immortality of the Victor through the principle of one body. I will introduce the Holy Dew Spirit which makes the followers of the great philosopher 'Super-Ego and Superhuman', the heaven of minds. The predictions of the Holy Dew Spirit, the hidden manna, in the Bible and the Buddhist scriptures were told in my collection of dissertations and 「The Secret of New Heaven'」. So you can see about the essence of the Holy Dew Spirit. Today I will show the pictures which heaven falls into the Idea World, which the eyes of humanity cannot see, I collected for 20 years while studying about the phenomenon of new religions. You can see the world of God through the pictures. Those who receive the Holy Dew Spirit experience heaven to be accomplished in their minds, feel the Idea World directly. How can we explain the secret of the metaphysical new heaven and the experience of the utopia in the ignorant worldly science which is under death. When people get out of consciousness of 'I', they can see the essence of new heaven according to Neo-humans

6) The Visible Idea World & the Culture and Philosophy of Neo-humans?

What is the Visible Idea World? Like the terms of linguistic philosophy, the invisible Idea World can be seen and experienced by the power of science and spiritual development. I first introduced the term as a philosophical term in the history of philosophy. So far, a lot of philosophers and ethnologists have insisted a transcendent existence or God invisible. However, the development of science and optics challenge to prove the essence of God, energy(氣), and spirit. Like this, the Visible Idea World which has been imagined abstractly and ideologically so far can be seen by the transcendent existence emits the light of wisdom and the immaterial world, opened the door of heaven, and revealed the essence of God. My thesis was possible because the transcendent existence revealed metaphysical phenomenon and I experienced it for 25 years. Due to the development of Astronomy, genetics, biotechnology, optics, the researches about the mystery of the universe and the essence of material are quietly done, so dichotomy of philosophical knowledge and the religious logic cannot lead the world. Now a study can have good result when it is progressed through the Holistic Ontological approach which philosophical thinking, and scientific methodologies, the other fields and so on join at researching. Like 1Corinthians 15:54 writes, "When the perishable has been clothed with the imperishable and the mortal with immortality, then the saying that is written will come true: "Death has been swallowed up in victory." And, at that time, people will see God face to face. Like the prediction of the Bible, due to the philosophy of life and the advent of Neo-humans who neither decay nor grow old and, people can experience the transcendent world which people did not feel. I will explain the result of my experiment of 20 years on the basis of the culture of immortality of Neo-humans.

7) The True Valuable Philosophy is the Philosophy of Immortality Which can give Salvation.

'The Han moum philosophy' and 'the philosophy of immortality is the philosophy which can save all humanity. If people practice the Han moum philosophy regarding everybody as my body, they cannot attempt desires or fight. There arenot wars or conflictions any more on the earth, robbers disappear, and policemen or soldiers who keep civilians or nations do not need any more. If people know that they were originally God, they will be reborn as the Holy Spirit, be good citizens, the border line will disappear, their minds' wall which regards everybody as other will collapse, and the world will become one. This campaign and the Han moum philosophy become the foundation of building new heaven which a lot of prophets dreamed. The Victor insisted that the Han moum philosophy is the philosophy of salvation and is the best way for the peace of the world, practicing is the share of all humanity. Where should philosophy go? To experience the essence of the utopia, the Idea World, the Visible Idea World, the direction of new study about the modern philosophy should be established.

First, philosophers should realize that right philosophy is started on the sane value, set a valuable philosophy.

Second, the direction of study to have to be preceded is that people should be open to the basic question about the essence of humanity and "who am I?" Third, the study of philosophy should start from the fact that humanity was originally immortal existence and light of wisdom, concentrate on investigating the cause for the result of present changed situation in causationism.

Fourth, philosophers should seek the Idea World not by their thinking or outside their body, but by listening to their conscience, observing their mind while judging and behaving as their conscience wants. All studies of philosophy and the changing of consciousness should be started at state removing of Ego, consciousness.

Fifth, the researchers should focus on the changing of their bodies and minds to the questions of seeking the essence and existence of God. Sixth, the study of the salvation of humanity, the scriptural and realistic definition of heaven, and the philosophical interpretation on the whereabouts of heaven should be done. Finally, they should study the methodology of immortal secret, the essence of the Han Moum Philosophy suggested by the Neo-humans. Also, the research on the Visible Idea World spiritual and metaphysical which has being built in the Neo-humans by the transcendent existence should be done as the subject of philosophy. In the Neo-humans who acquired the philosophy of immortality, heaven was built in them, and they live in the Idea World in accordance of my study of 20 years. It is the time when we first establish the Idea World in our heart. I hope that scholars will adopt the abovementioned suggestions when they study religion and philosophy.

Without mentioning 'Photon Belt', which, so-called, physicists and astronomies say, now it is the time of bright lamp, the era of brilliant light of the Sweet Dew, awaking persons will notice the secret of eternal life by studying it, feel heaven in their bodies and mind by practicing it, experience the essence of God. Also they will think that the Idea World which all philosophers have pursued is realized in their minds. Additionally, they will find Super Ego and feel it. They will find the clue that all humanity become one, are truly saved and free from death in the 'Han Moum Philosophy'. Furthermore, those who practice 'the Han Moum Philosophy' they will recover the original nature of humanity, reach the stage of God. In this respect, my thesis is important. Furthermore, I will introduce a new methodology which is suitable for studying a new theory or new transcendent phenomenon of new religion, I adopted while studying this philosophy. It will be an important methodology as approach when researchers study theology or religion. I adopted new methodologies as follows, studied through practicing, experiencing, and observation with researching the theories.

1. In the analyzing of data and the existing methodology of theologies, there are 'the collecting Holistic pieces' 'connecting factor and drawing pictures', 'finding pairing of homogeneity and fitting up' 'macroscopic combining observation', 'the way of standing an egg upright', 'combining and comparing many theologies', 'hidden metaphor silent observation, the way of realizing suddenly', and 'observation with transcendent spiritual eyes'.

2. In the methodology of metaphysical theology, the science of life, exploring experience of the scene of religion, going on an on-site survey', 'observation through experience', 'observation of self-experience and experiment'.

3. In the methodology of learning by experience in asceticism and practice, there are 'loving God looking at God's face', 'praying of destroying Satan with sitting up straight' (정좌관망 멸마기도법), 'returning to the nature by conceiving of the mind of retrogression' (복본역행포심법), 'being revived by destroying Ego' (멸아중생법), 'Overcoming self and returning to God giving affluent grace (극기복례법), 'removing pseudo consciousness' (가아투기제거법), Conceiving Self- conceiving self-sacrifice' (자기희생 포심법), 'finishing of pseudo consciousness martyrdom(가아 순교 임종법), 'Regarding neighbors as my body (애린여기 실천법). They are suitable as the methodology of be reborn as Neo- hu-

mans according to my study. I will explain new ways of asceticism and these methodology next time.

Now we came to know the role of philosophy, its limit, and the direction of the modern philosophy proceeding. And we also came to know the answer of what a valuable philosophy is. Therefore, the things we have to do is to realize that all humanity is one tree, one blood, one brother, and one body, to move the Ego which keeps people from knowing the essence of humanity and God, and to be reborn as the light of eternal life, the light of wisdom, and Holy Spirit. Like the Bible said, the philosophical wisdom to know God and the secret of heaven is possible by the pouring of the oil of the Holy Spirit, the rational ignorant spirit of humanity knows nothing, and the consciousness of 'I' cannot get out of the restraint of death. That was the secret and conclusion of the Bible. The Han Moum Philosophy is universal neither change or nor decay, which is the methodology of being reborn as the Neo-humans, by practicing it, 'the international Academy of Neo Human culture' and the Research Center of Neo-Humans want to share the practical methodology, the philosophy of new life science, with all humanity. Such practical tasks of the methodology of the philosophy of immortality are to realize the root of humanity, to keep the Law of Liberty, to conceive the mind of retrogression to recover humanity 's original nature, if humanity practice them, he can be reborn as immortal Neo- humans. This thought came to the world after Mr. Cho Hee Sung 曺熙星 overcame His Ego and death, I have studied the amazing new science through a practical methodology, arrange the philosophy of immortality as the Han Moum Philosophy, a new philosophy, and reveal it to the academic. Last, Socrates taught people "Be genuine to yourself", "Obligation to self is more important than that to

God or the Law." I want to say philosophers, topologists, and religionists "Like white paper, go to selfless, do not deceive your conscience, and act and think as your original nature wants.", "Be honest to your conscience", then the essence of the Ideal Form is revealed by itself and see you. And when they continue to focus on finding answer to the essence of humanity until seeking the brilliant light and being reborn as Neo-humans, the dream of humanity comes true on the earth.

Humanity is the branches of the tree of life. The tree of life is

CHAPTER IV
The Hidden Secrets of the Victor & the Final Issue of NRMs

God. But as Satan exists in humanity, they are God that is the slave of Satan. The consciousness of humanity was God but Satan permeated into Adam God and Eve God and occupied them. At the moment, they became humanity, since then, all humanity has died for 6000 years. The God among the Trinity God(God, Adam God and Eve God) developed the Holy Dew Spirit for 6000 years to dissipate the Satan in humanity. Therefore, if one receives the Holy Dew Spirit, Satan disappears, at the moment God becomes his/her consciousness, he/she will be changed into God. But they will not return to God of 6000 years ago, they will become stronger than the God in the beginning. The Victor has come to the world to make humanity Victors like himself. If people do not know the Victor and the secret of immortality, they can neither go to New Heaven nor receive salvation. Also, people do not know the hidden manna exactly, they cannot eat the fruit of life. The secret of the tree of life in Emerald Tablet is in this chapter. The secret of secrets of New Heaven of the God of Lord is the hidden manna, the man who has the hidden manna is the Victor; righteous man in the east

1. The Hidden Secrets of the Victor in the Bible
1) The Essence of Immanuel in the Bible

Isaiah predicted Immanuel. It means a man who God accompanies. Jesus stole the place of Immanuel. Only God becomes Immanuel and saves humanity according to 43:14. The New Testament says virgin Maria conceived Jesus. But the words of the Bible are spiritual. The virgin of the Bible is spiritual. The spiritual virgin is the man who opens the fifth seals; he is Park TaeSun, the creator of Jeondogwan, a religion, and the spiritual mother of Mr. Cho Hee Sung. He succeeded in producing Mr. Cho Hee Sung as a Victor with the Victress Eve. Gyeokamyourok records, 'Jeongdoryeong is the Holy Spirit, is a man who teaches right Dharma, and is the man who was accomplished as the Trinity.' 'He looks like a human but he is not human, but God.' The God in the beginning developed the Holy Dew Spirit for 6000 years that can makes humanity God and wore a body of humanity to save humanity by making them original God with the Holy Dew Spirit. The Bible records that God comes as a thief to the sons of dark, but the sons of light know the advent of God.

2) The Brief History of the Victory Altar

The Victory Altar started in Yeokgok dong Wonmi gu, Bucheon city on Aug 18th 1981. As on Aug 12th 1991, its 10th anniversary, its new building was completed in Yeokgok 3dong. It is a new earth by God, it became a burnt sacrificial altar where a lot of righteous men perform a ritual service to God every day, and it is a New Jerusalem. Gyeokamyourok predicted that Mr. Cho Hee Sung would build the Victory Altar and save humanity. Lee Ji ham foretold in his book「Gihaesangilseo」that Yeokgok is a winning earth(驛谷勝地). It is located in 175-2, Yeokgok 3 dong, Sosa Gu, Bucheon city, Gyeonggi province where the secret of the white stone was revealed.

The Victory Altar is where the Victor unifies Confucianism, Buddhism, and Taoism into one, and all humanity's dreams come true. The Victory Altar(勝利祭壇) is a short name for [Immortality Religion God's holy society the Victory Altar], the Victorious God is an existence that gives all humanity eternal life, it always descends in the Victory Altar. Let me tell you the role of the Victory Altar.

First it is not a kind of Christianity; but a place that the Victor God creates a new heaven and new earth. The truth of the Victory Altar combines not only Confucianism, Buddhism, and Taoism but also every religion into one. Soon this world will be unified into one in all aspects such as politics, economics, religions and so on. The splitting era will be finished by 'the wave of one', the principle of God. The work of unifying into one will be accomplished not by Western people but by Koreans, the chosen people. God, the essence of one, insists it Himself and does the work. The light of saving all humanity emits from the Victory Altar. As the Savior who will save all humanity is in the Victory Altar, the people of the world will eye the Victory Altar. When the light from the Savior shines, Korea will be the leader of the world in aspects of politics, economy, religions, and cultures. According to Isaiah 60 of the Bible and 桃符神人 part of Gyeokamyourok, all countries' people will come to Korea with gold, silver and treasures.

Second, the Victory Altar is where one practices the one body thought of regarding everyone as my body. This is because all humanity was made of their parents' blood, their parents' blood were made of their grandparents' blood, casting back like this, there comes the first ancestor.

Therefore, as all humanity is one body, we should regard everyone as my body. Comparing to a tree, all humanity is like a tree spreading with 7 billon branches, if a branch spreading to the east say to a branch spreading to the west, "you are not my body", it is very funny. Like that, all humanity is one body with the same blood vessel. So the Victory Altar is where one regards brothers' faults as mine, brothers' sin as mine.

Third, the Victory Altar is where the Sweet Dew(甘露) falls. The Sweet Dew is the Holy Dew Spirit, which can remove all sins in humanity and make them immortal.

If one receives the Dew, his/her body becomes clean and his/her diseases are cured, he/she becomes young gradually and finally becomes God. Let me tell you the system and doctrines of the Victory Altar. First, it is where the Savior teaches the way of immortality to humanity. Among humanity's hopes, eternal youth and eternity is the best hope. For this life, humanity has continually strived. The Bible talks about immortality "which God, who does not lie, promised before the beginning of time "(Titus1:2). The Victory Altar published a book 『A Farewell to Death』 and sent each president of over 120 countries in 1980s. More than 30 presidents reported out to show gratitude. At that time, eternal life was not familiar to them. Now is different. The Victory Altar is Mecca to announce the way of immortality and realize it.

3) The process of the Victor's reaching nirvana

The Victor, Mr. Cho Hee Sung' life was a sacrificial and struggling one against Himself. When He was in high school, He

helped His friends who did not go to school to go to school by making money at night. In the army, He taught soldiers who did not finish middle school or high school at day time, taught civilians at night and built 3 schools by Himself and made them public schools. Continuing hard work drove Him to the third step of consumption. He was cured in His dream by Mr. Pak TaeSun(the spiritual mother) who led Jeondogwan, religion, in Sosa. The next morning, He found there was two burnt hand print on His abdomen. His body was very good. So He went to a hospital and was x-rayed. His consumption was completely cured. That was their first meeting, but Mr. Cho Hee Sung did not know it. When He first met Mr. Pak TaeSun really not in a dream, he already knew that he cured Mr. Cho Hee Sung in His dream. As Mr. Cho Hee Sung recognized that God accompanied Mr. Pak TaeSun, He served Mr. Pak TaeSun as God, followed him. He drew his spirit by loving him highly and lived a life in contrast of what He wanted. He prayed without eating and sleeping for a month 14 times to kill His ego and draw the spirit of God. When He almost overcame Himself(ego), He was taken to the Secret Chamber in Sosa. There was the Victress Eve who God accompanied her. She read all the thoughts of people. He trained Mr. Cho Hee Sung to become a Victor. While living a life of objection 100 percent such as not sleeping when He was sleepy, not eating when He was hungry, loving person who hated Him, leaving Himself to God, He killed his ego(the spirit of death). That day is Oct 15TH, 1980. As the Satan in Him died completely, the Trinity God occupied His body and became a Victor. On that day, He went to a mountain to collect wood. The trees and grasses danced. The trees greeted bending their thick trunks and dance raising one branch up and the other branch down and grasses whose roots were planted in the ground danced up and down. As He told them to stop, they stopped their dancing. And he saw the grasses' roots were almost pulled on the ground. Mr. Cho Hee Sung spoke that He realized at the scene that He became a Victor.

4) The Mysterious Experience of neohumans in the Mandala World

The superb level is the taste of the final refining step of milk (mandala; the hidden manna)

Manda in mandala is the same meaning as [醍醐]. The term of 醍醐(Manda or Sarpir manda) is the taste of the last material when milk is refined. There are five steps in refining milk; milk(乳), lak(酪), immature step(生隣), mature(熟隣), and the final(醍醐). In Buddhism, people say that the taste of[醍醐] is the best, they compare its taste to nirvana. Finally, the milk of the final refining step is a kind of ghee in Sanskrit, it tastes like butter. However, the origin of the word is not sure, there is a saying that it came from old Mongolian that Indian people and old nomad used.

The milk of the final refining step is the best thing similar to

superb enlightenment. This is because of blood mixed with pyemia, people live with agony, the taste the final refining step is not the level of humans but nirvana. Also karma perishes, only ecstasy exists and can feel the nature of Buddha. Plus, as its taste is superb that karma completely perishes and only ecstasy and the nature of Buddha exist. Therefore, people named its taste superb one. This origin is written in the nature of the Reincarnate Maitreya Buddha 4-5 of the Great Nirvana Sutra, the superb taste of the Sweet Dew is the taste of the final refining steps of milk, it is the step of nirvana according to the Nirvana Sutra. Sakyamuni compared the nature of the Reincarnate Maitreya Buddha to the taste of the Sweet Dew. The Reincarnate Maitreya Buddha achieves superb enlightenment and achieves immortality, and the taste of the final refining steps of milk is a term of the qualification of the Reincarnate Maitreya Buddha after accomplishing the nature of Buddha. He dissipates the agony of people and cure people's diseases by emitting the Sweet Dew. Like that, the terms of nirvana, the Sweet Dew, three treasures, the Trinity Buddha are expressions in the world of Mandala. Also a similar term for the Mandala world is [醍醐], which is one of the core term in the secret Sutra of Buddha.

Mandala flower(曼陀羅華), flower rain, and 醍醐味 that symbolizes nirvana

According to the Amita Sutra, in the land of happiness, the Reincarnate Maitreya Buddha always stays as His other self, the infinite Sweet Dew and Mandala flower rain, which symbolizes nirvana and always falls down there. However, nobody talks about the Mandala flower rain. Therefore, I will introduce my enlightenment through the wisdom of the Sweet Dew using the term of Buddhism on the basis of the preaching of the Reincarnate Maitreya Buddha to save humanity in dark world. Mandala flower rain is the Sweet Dew in the land of happiness, it has the light of wisdom without any obstacles, it is the other selves of the Reincarnate Maitreya Buddha, and the Holy Dew Spirit.

Those who are lack in good character and are blind with sins and karma cannot see the Sweet Dew in the world of Mandala and cannot see things in advance. The Nirvana Sutra, the Dharma Lotus Sutra, and the Flower Adornment Sutra record that righteous men in immortal happy land see the Reincarnate Maitreya Buddha in their naked eye. Therefore, it is necessary to pay attention to the mysterious immortal world where people reach nirvana with their physical bodies in Sosa, Korea. The Buddhism Scriptures say that in the pure land Mandala flower rain falls down, people accomplish nirvana, the land is expressed as the Castle of the Sweet Dew, the door of the Sweet Dew, or Amita Palace. I examined a material to support the steps of achieving immortality of the Victory Altar, on the process, I found that the process of reaching nirvana of the holy group in the Victory Altar was already predicted in a secret Sutra, Sonbuljinsueorok (仙佛家眞修語錄), that has handed down through Buddhists secretly.

I said if people receive the light of wisdom from the Amita Buddha, they can achieve immortal bodies and the stage of nirvana. Now, let's examine what is the world of nirvana that last refined milk symbolizes?, what does the term of nirvana have relationship with the term of the last refined milk?, and what people should do to reach nirvana?There are four steps in explaining reaching the complete nirvana through cultivating themselves in the view of the kinds of expediential nirvana and comparing the refined milk with nirvana. Usually, the gist of sorting method is when people's levels grow up; they compare the degree of their mind and bodies becoming clean to the refining of milk. According to the Buddhist Sutra, there are four steps in the process of reaching nirvana. (1) The stage of achieving of Sudawon and Sadaham is small nirvana; its stage is like milk. (2) This stage is achieving of Ana ham, its stage is a middle nirvana, in this stage, people's blood is like stage that milk is through the second process refining. (3) This stage is called the holy saint, their blood is like clear alcohol (生酬)(4) When people are on the stage of righteous men or Sakyamuni, their stage is called great nirvana, their nature of Buddha and their blood is compared like 醍醐. The level of Buddha is like the Reincarnate Maitreya Buddha has infinite life span and He is an immortal existence that emits infinite light. He can change as a lump of fire anytime, also change into His other selves like tiny dirt. Anyway, the Nirvana Sutra compares the stage of achieving Buddha to the process of the final refining milk.

5) The Methodology of Practicing to reach Nirvana in the Mysterious Mandala World.

People should prepare to draw the life light in their mind.
 How to clean mind?
The most important thing for trainees for Dao is how to cultivate their mind, people can visit the Victory Altar for the methodology for practicing. I will introduce some crucial ways.
The first step for starting is stopping smoking, drinking, and sex because they make blood dirty that leads to death. Also for having clean mind and bodies, they should always take a shower. The process of twenty-one- education period, they should take worship services without one single day's skip. Also, people should not think of the past and they should forget

and empty their mind from common senses, knowledge, and experiences that they cannot see one inch in advance. Like that, they should prepare to receive new sayings and draw the light of life in new minds.

Do not distinguish between you and I
People should try to get rid of dichotomy that makes people conscious of each other. As all humans are one body, one blood, brothers and sisters, and one tree. We should throw ourselves, should not be conscious of ourselves, mash our existence, and get rid of it. And Satan has been in people's mind and mock, laugh at, and afflict humanity. Therefore, you should not forget that Tao is to remove the root of all kinds of evils related with I. That is, we should not throw away my habits and minds. Serve the Lord and lower yourselves all the time. As people do not know 'The Law of Liberty' that is a soap to clean mind and body, they die miserably.

It is necessary to lead a life sacrificial and yielding life, to regard others' fault as mine, others' sins as mine, forgive them, others' situation as mine, and others' pain as mine. Also, as this era is that of the Reincarnate Maitreya Buddha that the Sweet Dew falls, we should be convinced of immortality. Look at the Reincarnate Maitreya Buddha each second and adore Him highly

Finally, open mind and make an effort to look at the Reincarnate Maitreya Buddha every second and adore Him highly to have the qualification for having Buddha in mind all the time. Then the spirit of the Reincarnate Maitreya Buddha comes to you and makes you immortal ones. People think there are a lot of foods that clean blood and are good for health. However, the Sweet Dew is the best food that cleans mind and body. According to the Buddhist Scriptures, the best medicine cleaning mind and blood is the Sweet Dew that Reincarnate Maitreya Buddha pours down. Therefore, people should rely on, follow Him at the risk of life.

Overcome Yourself by Receiving the Sweet Dew

In conclusion, people's body is coexisted with Buddha's blood and the blood that causes agony. Like if milk is refined continually, the best taste is made, if we receive the Sweet Dew continually, our body and mind become clean, the Buddha's blood mixed dirty blood gets power and defeats Satan. If we have the mind of the Reincarnate Maitreya Buddha, the blood gets clean gradually and the mind reach nirvana that mind is so clean and has no agony.

If one's blood with agony is clarified by the Sweet Dew, the agony is removed, and his/her mind is changed like crystal. Then he can achieve the body and mind of Buddha that is unchangeable, does not rot, and become a light of life. People call it nirvana, consummator, and the nature of the Reincarnate Maitreya Buddha. That's because people compare the superb enlightenment to the best taste. Also another term for the perfect level of nirvana is the Sweet Dew. If people know the fact and try to seek the Reincarnate Maitreya Buddha in the Scriptures, they will know the secret and truth of the Reincarnate Maitreya Buddha and they will meet Him in Sosa(富川市素砂) Korea. Among those who try to cultivate themselves with three generations virtue, the men who achieve the level of righteous men can see the Reincarnate Maitreya Buddha with their naked eye and receive the chance of achieving the nature of Buddha.

6) Testimonies from New Earth, White Stone(SoSa= 素砂)

(1) Whojida Daheco(勝田多惠子)

Suddenly an illusion came to me. There was a huge desert under the blue sky. Foot prints of a man were connected in one thin line starting far away, which was stopped before me. Looking closely, it was only a trace on the line rather than foot prints. Somebody said that was my life's progress. I was surprised. I thought that fifty -year- varied life of one man left as a small trace on the sand, if a wind blows, it would be disappeared. At the moment, suddenly one wind blew and erased the trace on the sand for a second.

After winds blew, my illusion was disappeared. After waking up, I shed tears endlessly. Like a heroine who lost her past, did she feel a premonition that would happen? No, it was not. The wind played a beautiful music that I never heard, and I shed tears for being parted with loving and missed affection. I could not move at all. What is that reason? After that, I sometimes had an illusion, as time was passing, the interval was more frequently. One day I found a fact that the illusion came with a piano piece. When 'a piano piece called Eorian harps' was played by piano or harps, the illusions came to me. It was an odd titled song 'Harps that wind plays. I did not touch the piano or recorder. The training of God seemed like getting rid of beautiful, lovely, and favorable things of mine. And some time passed again. I felt captivated with fear strangely that something would come to me from God. After that time passed again. One day an old friend called me and we met. She talked about UFOs. It was my old interest. I just heard her story without saying my experiences. I parted with the friend doubting her intention who talked about old things. There was a call from her again. She said that a great teacher came from Korea. She continued the story again that she talked about before. Even though I was not interested in UFOs, not having appointments, considering the favor of my friend who did not know my experiences, I promised to participate the meeting again. "Korea and Japan are brother countries." That was the first saying from the Korean who talked to me first. I answered with mind. "Yes" He looked gentle. But his mind seemed gentler. Why did he come to Japan? I looked at the man's eyes. They looked pale which were suffering cataract. They were strange. I never met people who had holy eyes. His eyes looked holy rather than pale. I thought that he was a famous spiritual person. One of his followers, a Korean American, told me about his strong motivation to follow him. The man being called the Lord looked tired a little. After a little while, we watched preaching through a video with interpreting.

The interpreting began with "Human beings were originally God." It was the same saying with a traditional religion, Sindo (神道). I also agreed to the principle of blood. Furthermore, from the beginning, I was interested in the relationship between Korea and Sindo (神道) of Japan. I have believed Christianity since I was seventeen years old. I was interested in the similarity between Japanese Sindo and Israel history. I already knew that the offspring of Dan treaty came to Korea, one of the parts crossed to Japan. But I had thought that it had no relationship with Christianity. As my friend suggested me to go to Korea and take twenty-one lessons for beginners, I rejected it. When the Lord asked me to take the suggestion, I accepted it simply. I received a call from the friend again. He asked me if I was ready to go to Korea. It was not usual. I had the same experience in the past. The way chosen by God was just following only Him; throwing ones as mother, wife, and a man. Also I threw all things getting from the world. That day was my thirty-third birthday. The memory of the day came upon me. Will the affair happen again? Why need the affair now? What is this affair connected? After seven days since I met the Korean teacher, I already went to Korea. Even though I did not know the Victory Altar, my grateful life of twenty-one day lesson was started. I thought it would be a group for spiritual people. But it was different. Surprisingly its warship was like the form of Christianity. More surprisingly, Jesus was the object of His judgment. He was not conceived by the Holy Spirit as well as he was not crucified, either. He defected to France and lived to be eighty-four. So it does not make sense that he revived. Even though I have ever heard of it before coming to Korea, I ignored it due to not only having any evidence about that but also being others' religion. But the sayings that Jesus was neither conceived by the Holy Spirit nor crucified were conveyed by the Lord on the pulpit made me surprised. On the earth, who, whose will, by whose order, did the man say? I did not doubt the facts. Did He judge Jesus and reveal the God's will? There was a sign in front of the building. It says the Association of the World Eternal Life. Eternal life is to live forever. They shouted loudly eternal life to the world here. Then the Israel people who carried a heavy burden from Abraham who built an altar in Canaan came to Korea with God and repeated victories, built the Altar with the hero, and hold worship services to God now. Immortality is not only the last fruit of the Bible but also accomplishing the glory world without death and agonies in this land. 'Death is the wage of sins'. The last image of human beings is death. Will Jesus who taught eternal life after death come with objection with a thousand troops? Jesus was dead and was a sinner. Then who found immortality on the earth? Who is the Victor who proclaimed eternal life to the tremendous sinful history and stands after winning death?

He is just a gentle, humble, spiritual, and Korean man, said that Korea and Japan are brothers' countries. And also He is the humble and lofty Lord who found out the way of eternal life. He is the Savior who pours out the Holy Dew Spirit that God promised to give. Also He is the Reincarnated Maitreya Buddha with the Sweet Dew. The hero of prophecies, the man of heaven, Jeongdoryeong (the Savior who Koreans have waited for) comes as the same one person. Actually a surprising saying which men neither grow old nor die is accomplished in the Victory Altar in Korea. His sayings are verified. He is the beyond man who all the human beings have waited for. The work of saving life is accomplished in the Victory Altar in Yeokgok, Korea. At the moment people look at the Lord, their sins disappear. He is the super hero who destroys the elements of death. It is the surprising work of the Savior without shedding tears for washing sins and confessing sins. The day of collapsing Christianity will be accomplished soon. Thinking these huge affairs, I just shed tears. We will live with God. Actually He is a powerful and spiritual person. He came to me and made me be convinced of the Lord. Looking at the Lord, people's sins perish and they receive immortality. Those who listen to His saying even one time cannot help joining the work of new heaven. All the people of the world! the beautiful new heaven will be built soon. I am a witness who walks with the Lord, looks at the glory of the Lord, and lives with people conveying God's message to the world.

(2) Min Hae Kyeong

I went a Methodist church for one year before marriage. When I married, I knew that my husband went to (傳道舘) Jeondogwan led as sixth angel by Park Tae-Sun(朴泰善). At that time, as I went to a Methodist church without a special thought, at first I felt repulsion; I already went to Jeondogwan(傳道舘) in Yeongjudong following my husband.

One day in 1956, I smelt flagrance returning home after praying at dawn. I experienced that cooling grace that was connected from chest, abdomen, to arms. But I did not hear about the grace of live water, I thought that the phenomenon of receiving cool grace of live water was a kind of disease. So I went to a hospital, they did not know the reason exactly. Sometimes something hot came into by body, after some time passed; I came to know that it was the phenomenon of grace coming. But I moved to another area. Because my husband business failed, he lost his property. I was so shocked that my health went worse. Walking and carrying even one radish from a market were difficult. I went to a hospital, it was not helpful, and I came to give up life. One day Kim Soun-Ok asked me to meet a spiritual man. I accepted her suggestion, but I was too weak to walk. Trying to find out the way to meet Him, fortunately the man being called the Lord would come near my house the next day according to Kim Soon-Ok. At that time, the Lord was right after becoming a Victor; He did not do full-scale mission work. It was on October eleventh, 1981. My husband bought a month's Chinese medicine with left money; it was a desperate time to live or not. The next day two women being supposed to come and my party of three went into the man's room. Receiving grace in Jeondogwan for a long time, I knew the quality of energy that comes from people. The man being called the Lord told me to look at His eyes. So I saw His eyes. His eyes were emitting light. Being mysterious, I saw them continually. He asked me, "What will you do to catch a tiger? He told me that he became a Victor with looking at the Spiritual mother(Mr. Park TaekSun) without a second's missing. It made me think if I looked at the Victor, I would be like the Victor. Hence, as I continued looking at the Lord, He poured out the Dew Spirit to me. One day, I was on my way home after a worship service. My house was on the second floor. I used to take a rest two or three times going up the stairs. But on that day I felt my body was floating, and got to the floor of my house in a second. What made me surprised? Opening the door of my house, I found myself floating in the air. I was so excited that I tried to pick up a piece of paper to write a letter to my mother. But the paper flew up fast. Thinking it strange, I wrote a letter to my mother simply. And I went out of the room to change briquettes. The man (the Lord) giving me grace appeared there. And then He followed me continually. After taking a worship service, I was too happy and light, I could not see if I existed or not. People could not understand without experiencing this. At the beginning of going to the Victory Altar, my body was too heavy and sick, one day, during taking worship services, I felt a wind blowing on my head, surrounding my body, whirling, then a lump sized a fist in my stomach fell. At that time, the Lord told me to look at Him for the first time. At that time, I did not think that my disease could be cured. I was just curious about His eyes emitting light, so I followed Him unknowingly and saw continually. After that, things like a thread came from my eyes for two months. It was like a web. I thought it was an evil thing. There was continually a bad smell from my pee. It was my sins. Nowadays I am cured completely and go conveying God's message. When I send message, the holy Dew Spirit whirls my body, looking at the sky, the Lord is there. Every person looked as God. Babies looked as babies like the Lord, adults are adults like the Lord, and I realized the Lord's saying. As they actually looked as the Lord, I regarded them as the Lord. Rotten water looked like clean water of lake, dead trees looked like blooming trees, He made me heaven in my mind. If people receive grace, actually everything looks beautiful. It is not an illusion for a second. It is continued and real. I just try not to hurt people's mind, follow others' suggestion, and do nothing good, He gives me a lot of grace, I do not know how I pay back for His grace. If I talk about His grace with brothers, the Holy Dew Spirit comes to me. So I cannot help thinking the Lord. Like the Lord says, everybody is god. I cannot express all the grace of God minutely, it is just amazing. I think it makes a sinner God. I am writing this testimony to announce the advent of the Lord. Also I leave myself to the Lord giving huge grace to me at this moment.

(3) Monk Beop Sung, a Buddhist

The sins in my body disappeared with just looking the Lord
I have questions, "Where are human beings from, where do they go?" "What is the ultimate aim of life?" "Are human's life patterns fixed?" I have wondered about the above questions for a long time and thought that monks may know the answers about the questions. So I became a Buddhist of Myogak temple at the age of thirty-one. I tried to find out the true meaning of life. But I studied about life for several years, I could not find out the answers, and I was complicated instead with the various forms of Buddhism and languages. I saw several monks who were suffering with desire, anger and ignorance like worldly people and sticking to their self-respect and ego rather than piety from tenacity to find out the way to nirvana. I thought that monks had to live with a vacant mind coming from self-renunciation to realize the truth. But they looked like worldly

people wearing Buddhist monks' robe. When I felt that almost monks were the same as worldly people, I felt dejected. So I went to a small cave and started to meditate to make my mind empty. I tried to solve the question, "Even though all human beings are Buddha and the nature of Buddha is in everything, why do evils exist in them? How can I get rid of the evils in them?" Along the way, I was asked to run a building for propagation in Guabsa(甲寺). I could not reject the suggestion. So I became a monk for the building for propagation. Those who dropped by the propagation building looked like medieval people who wanted to go to heaven with indulgence. They prayed for their husband's promotion and their sons' pass to entrance exam after offering money to the Buddhist altar. Also people who worked at the propagation building were interested in only money. So I was disappointed at them, too. I tried to read books about Indian Yogi. I used to meditate after reading books which had the teachings of Rajneesh, Yoganada, and Maharishi. After three months in propagation building, BeobJeon monk came there. As he cultivated his moral sense in a cave for a long time, he looked calm. So I respected him from the first time. He said that the Reincarnated Maitreya Buddha appeared citing the Sutra of Lotus. He verified his saying using the Sutra of the Lotus. He explained the advent of Reincarnated Maitreya Buddha through the Buddhist books and 「Gyeokamyourok」 for several hours. After listening to his explaining, I was surprised by my childhood memories of a story about Jeongdoryeong. He said that Jeongdoryeong to make an immortal world appeared, the Jeongdoryeong is the Reincarnated Maitreya Buddha. So I followed him to Yeokgok where the Reincarnated Maitreya Buddha is. I was a little embarrassed about the building of the Victory Altar. It looked like a church rather than a temple. But I felt safe after listening that Reincarnated Maitreya Buddha was supposed to come from Christianity, unite Confucianism, Buddhism, and Christianity, and make all people immortal bodies. The form of worship service is similar to Christianity, they clap their hands during chanting. As I was accustomed to be in calm places in temples, I needed patience to follow the worship services. I found myself sticking to forms. I came to think if the man is the true Reincarnated Maitreya Buddha, just accomplishing nirvana is enough, whatever the form of worship service is, sticking the form of temples is not helpful to me. Thinking so, all my prejudice has gone, and I came to know that the form of the worship of the Victory Altar is better one. As I was clapping strongly, my entire distracting mind went away, the boundary between I and surroundings disappeared, only the Reincarnated Maitreya Buddha emitted light. Being surrounded by the light, I realized that I became one body with the Reincarnate Maitreya Buddha as light. As the Sweet Dew from Him dissipates all my sins, my body seemed like disappearing and became light like floating in the air. I knew the power of the Reincarnated Maitreya Buddha through the Sutra of Secret. Also I came to know from worship services that He had tremendous power to save all people from suffering for eternal cycle of birth and death. 'Human beings were Buddha who did not know death; Satan came into the Buddha with desires, angers, and ignorance. So human beings became mortal due to that. But their memory that they lived forever enjoying freedom remains in their blood; they try to find the way of reaching nirvana (their hometown) according to the Reincarnated Maitreya Buddha. He himself becomes a teacher, teaches the way of accomplishing eternal life exactly, and gets rid of bad mind (the soul of Satan) by pouring out the Sweet Dew. According to the Sutra of Secret, the Reincarnated Maitreya Buddha pours out the Sweet Dew, it goes into the pore of people, and makes people reach nirvana naturally. The Victory Altar where the Reincarnated Maitreya Buddha always resides has a lot of scents of lilies even in the bathroom. I came here to the Victory Altar due to the leading of BeobJeon. When he called to me to lead there first, I felt that strong energy came to the middle of the head. That was grace from the Reincarnated Maitreya Buddha. After about a month, I unlived the life of the propagation building and moved to the Victory Altar. Then I felt relief for coming to the place where I had to come. I felt friendly to the monks who already met the Reincarnated Maitreya Buddha. I am not realistic that I met the Reincarnated Maitreya Buddha. To meet the Reincarnated Maitreya Buddha is a big luck. I envied people who were born at the time of Sakyamuni and met him. But Now I met the Reincarnated Maitreya Buddha with much more power than Sakyamuni, I have no wishing now. How do I express my fullness of heart about meeting the Reincarnated Maitreya Buddha every day who removes all my sins by looking at Him. Entering university as top grade is good; getting a promotion is good, too. But luck that people meet the Reincarnated Maitreya Buddha and get out of birth and death is the best. Now is the time when I convey His message to the world. I will try my best in order for evils to be removed and for people to reach nirvana as soon as possible.

2. The Authority & Qualifications of the Victor

According to Revelation 2:26-28 in the Bible. "I will give the morning star to him who overcomes and does my will to the end; I will give authority over the nations. 'He will rule them with an iron scepter; he will dash them to pieces like pottery". It

means that God will give the Victor the name of 'bright star'. According to Revelation 2:7, "He will give the right to eat from the tree of life to him who overcomes." It means that the Victor is an immortal existence because he has the right to eat the fruit of life (immortal fruit).In Revelation 2:17, it says," God will give some of the hidden manna and a white stone with a new name written on it, known only to him who receives it." The Victor should give the hidden manna and know the name on the white stone. Revelation 3:12 says, "Him who overcomes, I will make a pillar in the temple of my God. Never again will he leave it. I will write on Him the name of my God, and the name of city of my God, the new Jerusalem, which is coming down out of heaven from my God; I will also write on Him my new name."
It means that the name of God is that of the Victor. That is, God is the Victor. Also Revelation 2:11 says," He who overcomes will not be hurt at all by the second death." It means that the Victor is an immortal existence. Revelation 3:21, "To him who overcomes, I will give the right to sit with on my throne, just as I sat down on God throne." It means God occupies the body of the Victor and becomes one with the Victor. That is, God is the Victor, the Victor is God. Like this, Revelation which is the last part of the Bible volume 66 says almost about the Victor, because if the Victor appears, immortality that is the aim of the Bible is expected to be accomplished. Therefore, God in John shouted the Victor to appear. Here what we should know is that the Victor, the Savior, and Israel indicate one person. As God is the Alpha and the Omega, God of the beginning was reborn as the God of consummation and became the Victor Savior and came to this world. The Savior is the man who was reborn as the Holy Spirit in Korea, the land in Far East corner like the prediction of Isaiah 41 1: 9. Putting the above words together,

Mr. Cho Hee Sung (曺熙星) who leads the Victory Altar in Yeokgok Bucheon city in Korea fulfilled above the conditions of the Bible. His name (熙星) means Bright star. He emits the hidden manna, the Holy Dew Spirit. Also as He received the white stone, He knows the name. He said the name is Sosa(素沙) 素 (so)means white, 沙 means a stone. In fact He built the Victory Altar in Sosa area in Bucheon city, Korea. As He received the power of God, He is almighty. Now I will show you His power. After He killed His ego(the spirit of Satan), He proclaimed the 5 public covenants for south Koreans in 1981.

The Mysterious Five Public Covenants which the Real Victor proclaimed

The Bible tells about God's existence and power through incidents. For example, God showed His power in Moses times. Like that, the Victor proclaimed five mysterious covenants in 1981 in Korea to show the people of the world that His power can change the mortal world into an immortal one. I will write about the five covenants that the Victor promised to Koreans. Five commitments of the Victor God are proclaimed to make foolish and doubtful men realize the existence of the Victor God. (The existence who overcame Satan is not God but the Victor God). Because God became the Victor God, He has had Almighty power. He proclaimed the five commitments to show doubtful people that He is a Savior. His commitments are as follows.

 1. I will remove Communism.
 2. I will halt monsoon rains in South Korea.
 3. I will keep South Korea from typhoons.
 4. I will make South Korean harvests abundant.
 5. I will prevent wars in Korea.

The five commitments were proclaimed on August eighteenth, 1981 by the Savior Jeongdoryeong, His promise has been kept for 31years. So South Korea becomes rich However, North Koreans have not been blessed by Him because they are against His will, so they have had a lot of floods and drought. Therefore, they are poor. All these things are the evidence of the Victor's His strategy to draw North Korea to the field of unifying the Korean peninsula.

Humans were originally God.
But in the beginning, the Trinity (Adam, Eve, God) lost a war against Satan. At the moment the Trinity lost to Satan, He became a captive; Adam became male, and Eve female. God being turned into male and female means that He lost the character of eternal life and was destined to die. The Bible says about this accident as follows: "Eating the forbidden fruit, they were driven from the Garden of Eden." And the books of Buddhism describe it 'because humans were shot by an arrow of three poisons; desire, anger, and ignorance, they were destined to die.' Also, at the moment the Trinity became the captive of Satan, He lost His omniscient and omnipotent power. Satan that captivated the Trinity God planned to annihilate the Trinity God. Its period is 6000 years, God and the universe were supposed to be automatically destroyed. But the Trinity God could not put up with the plan of Satan. God who was not caught by Satan succeeded in making the weapon of annihilating Satan by overcoming all hardship and adversity for 6000 years. And He appeared to the world to save humans wearing human's body. He is Mr. Cho Hee Sung; He appeared with the Holy Dew Spirit, the weapon of destroying Satan. On the day when God defeated Satan, mountains, streams, grasses, and trees danced, the sky and the earth cried with joy. In 6000 years, God overcame Satan in the mind of Mr. Cho Hee Sung, three God

who had been divided were combined into one body (Trinity), and became the Victor God. On October fifteenth, 1981, when God said to Mr. Cho Hee Sung, "You became a Victor ", He answered" I did not win, God won me." Finally three God became one body and recovered His omniscient and omnipotent power. And Cho Hee Sung proclaimed five commitments to announce His recovering Almighty power to the world in August, 1981. On the day when He revealed the five commitments, the sky trembled, and huge thunders rolled, and lightening flashed. What does it mean that the sky and the ground answered and God was happy? At that time, the Victor Savior, Mr. Cho Hee Sung said, "because the children of God have died for 6000 years, God has been very sad, now the will of God is accomplished. Until now there was neither heaven, nor the Garden of Eden, nor the fruit of life, nor righteousness. So, nothing good was to God. God has served as a slave to Satan for 6000 years." Like this, the wish of God who has lived in a miserable situation as a captive of Satan has been accomplished in 6000 years and recovered His omniscient and omnipotent power through Cho Hee Sung. The Victor, Cho Hee Sung, said like this " Self-consciousness of 'I' , Satan, has controlled God for 6000 years, but the great Victor who kills Self-consciousness of 'I', the Satan, appeared in Korea today. The Victor is not a man. As God killed the Satan (His Self-consciousness) of Cho Hee Sung, occupied His body, and became a victor, the Victor is the Creator God. The Creator God strategically deprived the royal authority of Satan, which controlled the universe for 6000 years, and occupied the crown.

The Holy Dew Spirit uses the omniscient and omnipotent power. The Five commitments show that the Trinity God has recovered His omniscient and omnipotent power. The Victor God proclaimed the five commitments to show that He governs the whole universe. The five commitments mean that He became the Victor on October fifteenth, 1981, snatched the authority of controlling the universe, and recovered His royal authority. Let me introduce His words. "A long time ago, as Satan occupied space, God did not have any power. But after God killed the Satan, and He recovered and exercise His Almighty power." The Victor God who appeared as the Savior controls winds and clouds as He wants according to 「Gyeokamyourok」. The Savior, a true man, uses the power of controlling wind and cloud as He wants, according to Revelation 11:6, "He closes the door of heaven and He will halt raining using His power during the predicting period" The Five commitments have been accomplished.

Commitment 1 " He will remove communism".

It was accomplished. He appointed Gorbachev as the president of Soviet Union and changed all the communism countries in the world into democratic countries. In August, 1991, a civilian revolution that was recorded as the greatest revolution in the human history happened in the Soviet Union, the birthplace of Communism. The great revolution of the century that announced the end of communist dictatorship was that of reform which was expressed as 'Perestroika' of Mikhail Gorvachev, the president of the Soviet Union. Nobody knows that it was the Trinity Victor who removed Communism, which was supported by more than half the number of countries on the earth. The Victor Cho Hee Sung proclaimed that He would eradicate Communism in 1981 when Communism was prevalent. Communism is an ideology that separates between parents and their friends; it cannot disappear suddenly in one day. The Victor who is Almighty and has the power of controlling the mind of people set Gorvachev, a person of the same age as the Victor His age, at the head; He revised the mind of the Soviet Union people through Gorvachev and made him control the mind of all the leaders of communism. On the day when the coup of some communists was failed, there was a rainbow over the Victory Altar on a sunny day.

The daily record of Communism's collapsing

    1985.3.11, Gorvachev was chosen as the leader of the Soviet Union, Communism adopted the line of reformation

    1986. 07.28, the declaring of Vladivostok, which created the mood of thaw in Asia-Pacific area

    1987.6, the permission of the pursuit of profit, the reformation of economy

    1988.03.19, the declaring of new Beograd

    1989.08.12, the collapsing of Communism in the east Europe without intervening of the Soviet Union

    1990.09.25, the Soviet was adopted the comprehensive market economy.

    1991.4.1, the Warsaw Treaty Organization was disbanded.

    1991.06.16, Yeltsin declared the collapsing of Communism.

    1991.06.28, COMECON was disbanded.

    1991 08.12, Yeltsin reorganized the administration excluding Communist

    1991.08,20, Gorbachev lost his position

    1991.08.22, Yeltsin arrested the persons who led the coup

    1991.08.26, Communism was disbanded

When the Victor, Mr. Cho Hee Sung, set Gorbachev at the head and controlled him to destroy Communism, on August twentieth, 1991, existing central communists who objected the disbanding of Communism caused a coup and imprisoned Gorvachev. At that time, the people of the world thought that the dissolution of Communism would be failed. So they were nervous and worried. But on August twenty - first, 1991, the Victor, Mr. Cho Hee Sung, announced on the pulpit of the Victory Altar "Gorvachev will be free soon." The Victor, Mr. Cho Hee Sung said, "He appeared in front of the communists who imprisoned Gorbachev, at that time the body of the Victor was as big as a house according to the Victor, actually He can change His body as He wants. The Victor yelled at them "Unless you release Gorbachev, you will die." And they were scared and ran away. So nobody was there, Gorbachev came out of the room without knowing the situation. After Gorbachev was released, on August twenty - second, 1991, Yeltsin arrested the people who led the coup, on August twenty - third, 1991; he organized the leadership excluding communism. Like this, the Victor announced the people of the world the breakup of Communism without revealing Himself. Also to reveal the hero of the breakup of Communism, He made twin rainbows be over the Victory Altar on a sunny day around five pm. on August twenty - third, 1991. The disbanding of Communism was the splendid achievement of God that eradicated the plan of Satan that would annihilate all humans.

Communism centering the Soviet Union and democracy centering America were facing each other in a cold era. The tense fighting of both camps drove the world into horror. It would be the third world war. The nuclear weapons which America and the Soviet Union reserved were the amount which could destroy the earth twenty times. In this situation, if the third world war breaks out, it will destroy the earth completely and life will not exist anymore. Therefore, the Victor, Mr. Cho Hee Sung's accomplishment of the disbanding Communism is huge work to save humans from a nuclear war. Nostradamus of France, a greatest prophet, said, in 「Morden centuries」 "The earth would be destroyed in August, 1999." Accordingly the people of the world are worried. When the Victor Savior proclaimed that He would eradicate Communism, people laughed at Him at that time. But thirteen years since He proclaimed, He eradicated Communism completely from the earth. The word of the third world war has disappeared completely. The accomplishing of the Victor's first commitment 'removing Communism' eradicated the basic root of humans' horror, and it is a great achievement to save humans. Here are the important evidences to support that the Victor broke communism. Kenani Gera Simof, the spokesman of Kremlin, said on TV as the ambassador of the Soviet Union in Lisbon " A changing started in Communism world from 1981" Also Gorbachev said, " The breakup of Communism was his terrible mistake." Mikhail Gorbachev won a Novel Peace Prize due to the finishing Communism. Like Mr. Cho Hee Sung said, after Gorbachev was free, there was a rainbow over the Victory Altar to show that the hero who removed communism is in the Victory Altar. Rainbow means the commitment of God. The bright part by the rainbow is the Holy Dew Spirit, which is the Spirit of Victor. This is the evidence that Mr. Cho Hee Sung released Gorbachev. Gorbachev eased off the arms race by pursuing the reformation of Perestroika. However he said, "The disbanding Communism was a terrible mistake" in an interview with a reporter of the Chinese Communism official organ, People's Daily newspaper on June second, 2006. How will you interpret his recalling the past? We can see that the disbanding Communism was not his thought, but he did it by not his intention. The Victor, Mr. Cho Hee Sung, used Gorbachev, a person of the same age as the Victor, as regent to accomplish His will and made Gorbachev remove Communism. Mr. Cho split Himself into billions' other selves and went into the each Communist, and rooted out the ideology of Communism in them. Other existence that Nostradamus said saved the earth. While Nostradamus talked with Queen Catherine about the existence of salvation, she asked 'who would appear on doomsday', 'whether people could avoid the doomsday', 'whether people should just wait for the day without any trying', 'whether God or angels help people' 'Is there any ways for salvation?' Then Nostradamus answered "No. There is no way for salvation. People cannot avoid the collapse. That is destined to them in that time. But I think if other existence appears, terrible circumstance of the doomsday will disappear. I do not know because it is in the mist far away. I do not know, either if it appears to me." The above words mean that all humans do not escape the destruction in dooms day. However, if other existence appears, they can avoid the terrible circumstance. The other existence is just the Victor, Mr. Cho Hee Sung. As the Victor, Mr. Cho Hee Sung, appears as a Victor, to proclaim the removing of Communism showed His will that He would eradicate the basic root of humans' horror, Satan's plan; the doomsday of the earth.

Commitment 2 "He will halt monsoon rains in South Korea."

It has been accomplished for 31 years.

Korea Meteorological Administration revealed "They will not use the term of monsoon rains" Monsoon rains disappeared. Mr. Cho Hee Sung was born as a son of a poor farmer. Korea had monsoon rains every year, they caused poor harvests. He was so sorry to see hungry people. So He thought if He halts monsoon rains, Koreans will be rich. Hence He proclaimed that He would halt monsoon rains in Korea. And of course it has been accomplished for 31 years. Monsoon rains are ones from June

fifteenth to July fifteenth. From old times, Korea had a lot of rains without stopping from June fifteenth to July fifteenth every year. They ruined harvests. People called the rains of the period 'monsoon rains'. Like that, the monsoon rains ruined rice, Koreans' staple, so the monsoon rains became the reason of poor harvests. But in August, 1981, since The Victor, Mr. Cho Hee Sung proclaimed that He would halt monsoon rains in South Korea, monsoon rains have not fallen in that period. Hence the Korean Meteorological Administration used new terms to call 'the period of no long rainy seasons' such as 'dried monsoon rains', 'monsoon rains without raining', and 'guerrilla monsoon rains' according to the newspaper ChoSunIlBo of August twenty-third, 2008. Namely, the rains falls a little, stops, and disappears; it is monsoon rains not like monsoon rains. Even though monsoon rains season comes, no monsoon rains, after the period, it rains a lot. As the Korean Meteorological Administration's weather forecasts have been off for twenty - eighty years, they were denounced by all Korean people, so they revealed that they would not tell the monsoon rains officially.
Mr. Cho Hee Sung halts monsoon rains.
Until the Korean Meteorological Administration reveals the article, they were criticized a lot through public opinion. As the Victor, Mr. Cho Hee Sung, controls the weather with His Almighty power, the weather forecast cannot be right. Like that, Mr. Cho Hee Sung's covenant "He will halt monsoon rains" has been accomplished completely.

Commitment 3. He will prevent Korea from typhoons.
Before 1981, Koreans had poor harvests due to more than twenty typhoons every year, and there were a lot of victims and damages from them. But since 1981, typhoons have been disappeared or suddenly changed their courses before the Korean

peninsula or perished; there have been the phenomenon of typhoons missing, which is incomprehensible to ordinary people. Daily Sports newspaper of August twelfth, 1988 put the title "Typhoons, which are summer's unwelcome guest, are missing" and "the courses of nine typhoons were changed avoiding Korea or perished" on a small title.

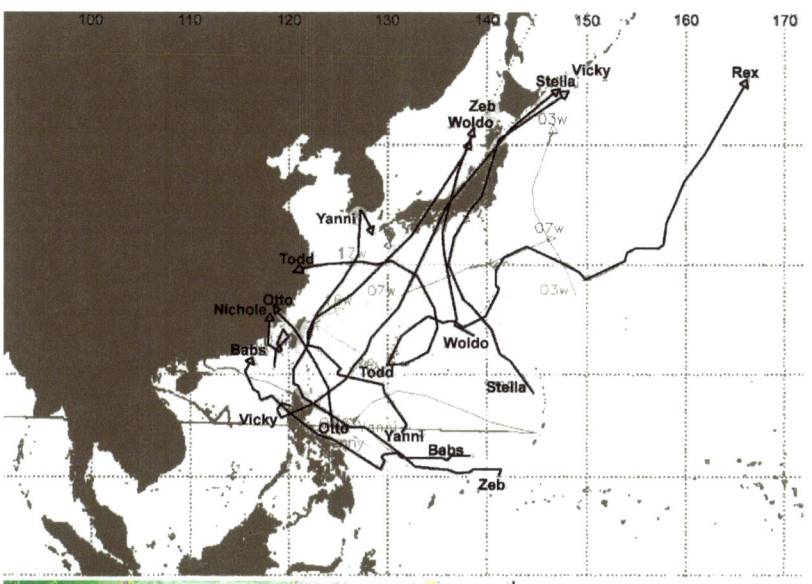

They loaded an illustration of nine typhoons, which came toward Korea and evaded Korea. They added "continuing hot summer weather is not unrelated with the missing of summer's unwelcomed guest, typhoons. Will such typhoons really disappear this summer? Korea usually has one or two typhoons by this time every year. But this year, there is no sign for typhoons. It is not because typhoons have not formed in the pacific, they are turned to the Philippines or China, and so they do not affect Korea." In 2009, typhoons gave tremendous damages to Japan, Taiwan, and China, but Korea did not have any typhoons, although it is located between them. The Victor, Mr. Cho Hee Sung's promise "He will keep Korea free from typhoons" has been accomplished. Therefore, Korea is a country blessed from the Victor, God.

Commitment 4. "He will make Korean harvests abundant. Korea has had abundant harvests for 31 years." Korea had one or two year's good harvests, and then one year's bad harvest periodically. So there was a term of 'barley hump'. Hungry people were looking forward the period of barley harvest. Korean people were hungry ones. Even though the decrease of rice planting area has occurred, abundant harvest has continued for 31years. But from 1981, the rice planting area has been declined five percent every year due to the exodus of young adults from agricultural areas, however abundant harvests have continued; it is surprising. To have abundant harvests, farmers need enough sunshine, water, and no damage by diseases and insects of rice etc. In other words, unless heaven helps farmers, they never have abundant harvests. Thanks to the Victor, Mr. Cho Hee Sung, Koreans have had abundant harvests for 31years. This must be blessing from heaven.

Since Mr. Cho Hee Sung promised the five covenants, the amount of production of rice has been growing rapidly; there is no year that does not have three hundred tons of rice harvest. It means that Korea has had abundant harvests every year. Because of continuing good harvest, the government had a problem in storing it, so it asked farmers to cut down the production of rice.

Korea is a small land, but North Korea, the north part of 38parallel, has a different situation from South Korea. It has had bad harvests due to continuing droughts or floods, so there are many people dying of hunger. It is sad for South Koreans to think of them. Anyway, the Victor's promise to make Korean harvests abundant has been accomplished for 31years.

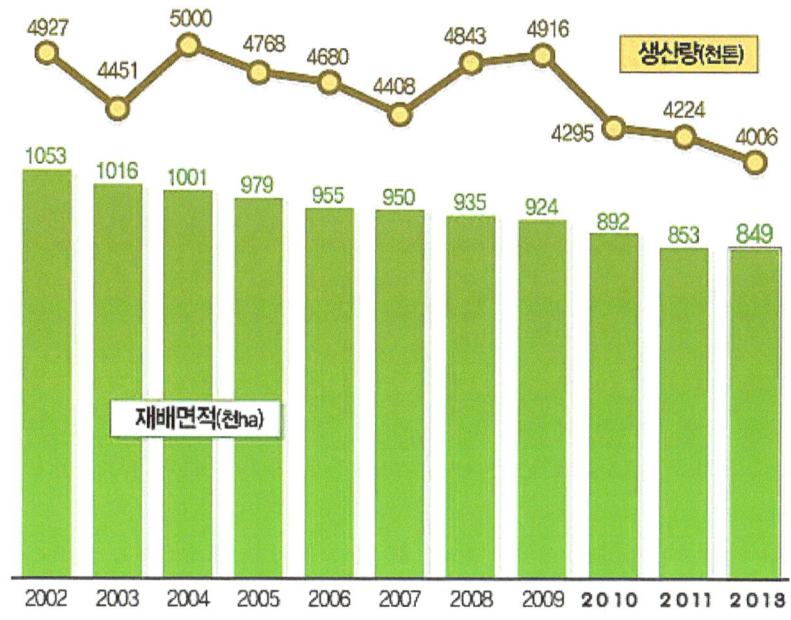

The production of rice from 1981 to 2006

Commitment 5. He will prevent Korea from wars.

Nobody forgot the pains of Korean War in1950. It caused not only two million casualties and death but also tremendous damages of property. Accordingly Korea became a heap of ashes and the poorest country in the world. People think if the second Korean War breaks out, it will be beyond the local war, it will be expanded to the world war, and then the world will face the destruction of humans. The Victor proclaimed that He would prevent wars in Korea. He provided an institutional strategy for wars not to break out in Korea. North Korea does not give up the illusion of unification by military force, but since the Victor's promise, the condition of institutional strategy is set to deter occurring wars. He made both South Korea and North Korea joined UN. Above all, North Korea's joining UN earlier than South Korea is eccentric. The South North Korea led a reconciliation mood by making peaceful atmosphere between South Korea and North Korea, they decided not to attack each other and exchange cultures from the fifth meeting of high officials at the meeting from December tenth to December thirteenth of 1991 in Seoul. The Victor made Kim Dae Jung the president of South Korea and thought about the reunification of Korean peninsula. In 1997 when the Victor served time in jail, His some went to the jail to meet Him. He said, "The president of this election will be Kim Dae Jung." They doubted to hear that because, at that time, people thought that Lee Hoi Chang, the counterpart of Kim Dae Jung, would be elected. But the Victor said that Kim Dae Jung candidate would be a new president. Above all, He said that He would put up Kim candidate as a president of reunification. One day, a few days before the election, Mr. Cho in the prison ordered some seniors of the Victory Altar to go to Kim Dae Jung candidate's house to say to him that "Kim Dae Jung will become the president of South Korea. "So some seniors of the Victory Altar went to Kim Dae Jung candidate's house with a towel on the day before the Election Day.

The towel embroidered with a wriggling dragon said, "Congratulations on being elected as the president. At that time, Kim Dae Jung candidate was moved deeply and appreciated Him. As the Victor said before the election, "Kim Dae Jung was elected as the president of South Korea", His plan, 'keeping Korea free from wars, was progressed well as planned. The government of Kim Dae Jung regarded inter-Korean relationship very highly. He considerably changed the relationship of two governments strained for last fifty years. The two governments have been close through the sunshine policy of South Korea. On June fifteenth, 2000, Kim Dae Jung, the president of South Korea, visited North Korea and held the summit in a peaceful mood, and achieved the joint communique of June fifteenth between South and North of Korea. Starting to send 1000 cows to North Korea, opening tourism to Geumgang Mountain, they made a great progress in exchanging economics & culture. The sunshine policy of the Kim Dae Jung government contributed to the peace of Korean peninsula. And also the government drew firm support from four strong countries; America, Russia, China, and Japanese, which did not trust the former government of Kim Young Sam. Therefore, he won a Nobel Peace prize. Here are some developments that made the Korean peninsula peaceful. In June, 2000, not only Koreans but also people around the world watched Kim Dae Jung, the president of South Korea, visiting North Korea for the first time. The holding of two leaders in Sunhang airport of North Korea made people excited. The two governments agreed to connect Gyeongui railway and Dounghae one, they started to open the road in 2003, and Gyeongui railway in 2007. And also the reunions of separated family were accomplished. The Victor Mr. Cho Hee Sung paved the groundwork in order for Korean Wars not to break out. Until now the Victor has deterred wars. Also His commitment, which He will prevent wars in Korea, has been accomplished. The Victor proclaimed the five covenants as I said above, Isaiah prophesied, thousands years ago, that the Victor would appear and accomplish the affair of heaven. Also in Genesis in the Bible, it predicted that the Savior would come from the tribe of Dan, the fifth son of Jacob of Israel. Jacob predicted the future of 12 branches; he predicts a little about Dan's future, because God hid the tribe, who would produce the Savior from Israelites. Nowadays the Dan tribe is lost one; so Israelites are looking for them. Therefore, next I will explain about the lost tribe, God's secret plans and strategies.

3.The secret of Lost Tribe, Dan is Korean

This contents are extracted my book「The Secret of New Heaven」 The researchers of the Bible think that the Savior was from Judah or will come from Judah. However, the Bible writes in detail about from what tribe the Savior comes. The words of the Bible are prophetic and spiritual, they are written in order for the chosen people to interpret the Bible. In Korea, the Victor has revealed the secret of heaven in the Bible for 30 years. I came to know the essence of the Victor and the lost tribe through the Bible and have studied for 20 years the secrets of heaven and the lost Dan tribe which were revealed by the Victor. What is the secret of the Hebrew on the roof-end tiles found in the bank of the Deadong River(大同江)?The Victor Savior, Cho Hee-Sung, revealed the secret of the roof-end tiles which were found in the Deadong riverbank in Korea. Do you know the amazing fact that the roof-end tiles that were found in bank of the Deadong River have ancient Hebrew on them? The roof-end tiles, which renowned archaeologists did not know, will change Korean history completely. In spite the fact has come out through several publications for twenty years, why did they not come into the spotlight to people? Among the twelve tribes of Israel, Dan who led the Dan tribe is just the founder of Korea, so Korean history is about 3000 years. The Savior Cho Hee-Sung knew that, not by human's ability but by the power of God, He has insisted on changing Korean history correctly. Renowned scholars of Korean and Israel confirmed that the patterns on the roof-end tiles are ancient Hebrew. The Savior Cho Hee Sung said that Korean people are Dan tribe of Israel. That evidence is the Hebrew on the roof-end tiles which were found in the bank of the Deadong River in Korea. The Victor told some young men to go to the Seoul National Museum, to take pictures of the roof-end tiles, and to take them to Sin Sa-Hun, who was a professor of Seoul National University and expert in old Hebrew. The professor confirmed that the patterns on the roof-end tiles are ancient Hebrew. I went as a reporter of KTN(Korea Travel News) to Israel to confirm the Hebrew on the roof-end tiles. I met Mr. Ed. Greenstein, a professor of Bar ILan University there. Ed. Greenstein told that the Hebrew on the roof-end tiles is BC late

고대 히브리어가 새겨진 와당 (The roof-end tile with the ancient Hebrew)

* 시대 : 고구려 5~7세기 (Age of Goguryeo, 5th~7th c.)
* 출토 지역 : 평양 대동강 유역 (Daedong river valley, Pyongyang)
* 전시실 : 국립 중앙박물관 이우치 이사오 기증 유물전시실
  Exhibit Hall : Iuchi Isao Collection in the National Meseum of Korea

1987년, 이우치 이사오 선생님이 유물 1,082점을 국립중앙박물관에 기증하셨다. 평생동안 직접 모으신 고대 한국의 벽돌이나 기와 중에, 고대 히브리어가 새겨진 와당이 있다.
In 1987, Iuchi Isao(1911-1992), a Japanese collector, generously presented the National Museum of Korea with a total of 1,082 items of bricks and roof tiles to promote friendly relations between Korea and Japan. Some roof-end tiles carved with ancient Hebrew.

히브리어 해석(decipher the writing on the roof-end tile)

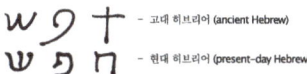

- 고대 히브리어 (ancient Hebrew)
- 현대 히브리어 (present-day Hebrew)

* 뜻 : '도착했다' (This means 'arrived')
* 해석자 : 고 신사훈 박사 (전 서울대학교 종교학과 교수, 히브리어 전문가)
  Translator : Dr. ShinSaHoon (Hebrew expert, the former Professor of Religious Study in the Seoul National University)

8~6 century. Here are their interpretations about the Hebrew of the roof-end tiles.

The interpretation of Mr. Ed Greenstein about the roof-end tile ① is the same as the interpretation of Mr. Sin Sa-Hun. Both of them interpreted it as 'arrive'

The picture of roof-end tile ② has a pattern of five leaves, Hebrews meaning 'a knot', 'the Kingdom of God', and 'enter'. The roof-end tile ② tells "Go to the Kingdom of God by becoming one with the Savior(the flower of five leaves means an everlasting life and the Savior).

The interpretation of the Hebrew of roof-end tile ② of two professors is almost the same. Mr. Ed Greenstein reinterpreted 'Knot, Conspiracy' as becoming one, by pulling together', Mr. Sin Sa-Hun as 'cooperate'.

< The roof-end tile with the ancient Hebrew >

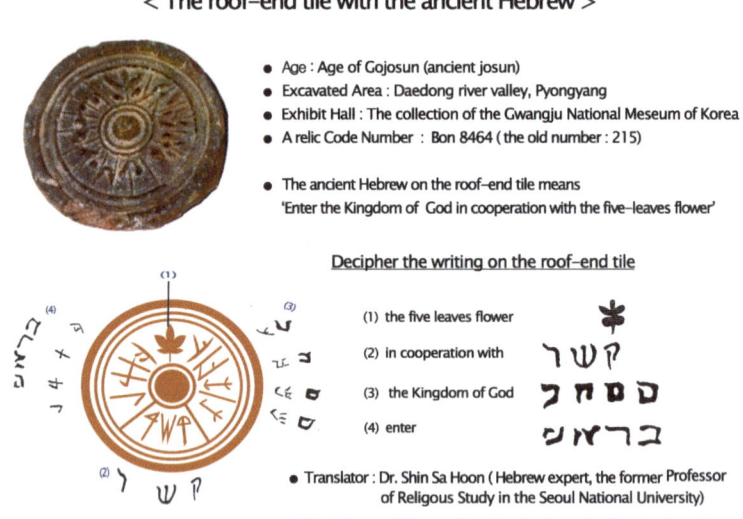

- Age : Age of Gojosun (ancient josun)
- Excavated Area : Daedong river valley, Pyongyang
- Exhibit Hall : The collection of the Gwangju National Meseum of Korea
- A relic Code Number : Bon 8464 (the old number : 215)
- The ancient Hebrew on the roof-end tile means
  'Enter the Kingdom of God in cooperation with the five-leaves flower'

Decipher the writing on the roof-end tile

(1) the five leaves flower
(2) in cooperation with
(3) the Kingdom of God
(4) enter

- Translator : Dr. Shin Sa Hoon (Hebrew expert, the former Professor of Religous Study in the Seoul National University)

< The informer : The society of archeology & cultural anthropology >

Professor Ed Greenstein interpreted the left Hebrew of roof-end tile ③ as "please turn around the flock of sheep", the right

Hebrew of roof-end tile ③ as "The ruler has commanded the law of liberty of a ruler". The interpretation of the Hebrews on the right side of roof-end tile ③ is almost the same as professor Sin Sa-Hun's too.

< The roof-end tile with the ancient Hebrew >

- Age : Age of Gojosun(ancient josun)
- Excavated Area : Daedong river valley, Pyongyang
- Exhibit Hall : Iuchi Isao Collection in the National Meseum of Korea
- A relic Number : Jungnae 124 (the old Number : 226)

  The ancient Hebrew means ' The judge governs with the proverb'
  'The heaven will be recovered by saint's prayer'
- Translator : Dr. Shin Sa Hoon (Hebrew expert, the former Professor of Religious Study at the Seoul National University)

Decipher the writing on the roof-end tile

This means 'The judge governs with the proverb'   This means 'The heaven will be recovered by saint's prayer'

 Sin Sa-Hun interpreted the Hebrew of roof-end tile③ as "The heaven will be recovered by saints' prayer." "The Judge who teaches the proverb governs." Judging from the Bible and the words of the Victor, the Hebrew of the roof-end tiles③ mean "go back to the white flock in the New Heaven and the New Jerusalem", 'the proverb' is the Law of Liberty which makes people be reborn as the Holy Dew Spirit, 'the ruler' is the Victor, the righteous man of the east, who tells the Law of Liberty and pours down the hidden manna to the flock of sheep meaning the white flock(Holy saints), and governs the world as His other selves. The roof-end tiles that have been placed in the Korean National Museum say that Koreans are the chosen people, Israelites.

However, Korean people do not know the root of Korean exactly yet. They have been told that their grandfather is Dangun(檀君), whose mother was a bear and was reincarnated by eating garlic and wormwood. But the Savior said the root of Koreans is Israelites, Dan-gun is the fifth son among Jacob's twelve sons. (gun means a king, it is a suffix for honorific title, Koreans still put gun behind family name.)

Who is Dan tribe?
The Holy Spirit of Lord who accompanied Abraham moved to Isaac, who the first wife of Abraham delivered at her age 100 years according to Genesis in the Bible. And the God of Isaac who accompanied as Holy dew spirit moved to Jacob, the God of Jacob moved to not Judas but Dan according to the Bible (Genesis 27:27, 49:16). 'Dan' is Hebrew, it means 'judge'. Judgment is the authority of the Victor Savior. The Bible surely says the Victor Savior will come from the Dan tribe.

The reason that Hidden Dan tribe came to Korea
Only the Savior who God accompanies knows the reason that God sent only the Dan tribe among the twelve tribes of Israel to the northeast. As God has been with the Dan tribe of Israel, God knew in advance if the Dan tribe stayed in Canaan, they would be perished by other tribes. So the God of Lord picked up the Dan tribe from Canaan and moved them to the Korean Peninsula where the sun rises, the Farthest East. The reason Israel people were persecuted and massacred by Mussolini, Stalin, and Hitler was because of Satan's plan. Satan tried to wipe off the Israel people completely. Because he knew that the Savior would appear from them. Therefore, God hid the Dan tribe in Korea far away from the area without anybody's notice and He raised the Dan tribe with the aim to bring up the Victor.

The route of the Dan tribe's immigration to the Korean Penin-

sula

The Dan tribe was placed at Zora between Jerusalem and Tel Aviv and fought against the Philistines for hundreds years. Dying Captain Samson by the Philistines, the Dan tribe lost a will to fight and started to move to the northeast 3000 years before the North Israel collapsed. After that, the Dan tribe disappeared completely in the Bible. However, the Savior knows the rout of the Dan tribe's moving to the Korean peninsula by the spiritual power of God because God of the Lord who directly led the hidden Dan tribe to Korea accompanies the Savior. According to the Victor Savior in the Victory Altar(SeungRiJeDan), the hidden Dan tribe left Zora of Israel, moved to Dan area nearby northeastern of Lebanon and lived there for a while, moved to Syria, Iraq, and Iran; they stayed in the Altai Mountains for around 100 years. The old generation died there, the second generation grew up, accustomed there, and learned Altai language to survive. So they forgot Hebrew gradually. After that, the Dan tribe crossed over Altai Mountains, lived in Mongolia. However, the main people of Dan tribe moved to the south, passed Manchuria, crossed the Abrok River(鴨綠江), and arrived at the Korean Peninsula. They settled on the Deadong riverbank and founded Gochosen(古朝鮮), the first government of Korea 2800-2600 years ago. So Mr. Ed Greenstein's decoding that the Hebrew of the roof-end tiles is that of late BC 8 century - 6century coincides with the words of the Victor Cho. Here is another story about ancient Hebrew. According to Mr. Go Jeong-Rok who worked for Korean independence, while his father was logging in Baekdoo Mountain(白頭山) in North Korea, he saw Dan memorial stone(檀君誌石) there during the colonial period of Japan. Some letters were engraved on it; they were neither Chinese nor Korean. So nobody decoded it. Fortunately, in those days there was a French catholic priest who studied old Hebrew. He decoded it. The strange old letters were ancient Hebrew; he said that the memorial stone was made around 3000 years ago. At that time, nobody understood why the memorial stone of Dan was written in Hebrew. Unfortunately the memorial stone was taken by Japanese; so we do not know where it is.

*The Dan tribe will judge his people
The general public says that the Savior will come out from the Judas tribe and will save humans. However, this is wrong. According to the Bible the judge Savior was supposed to appear from the Dan tribe and to judge all humans including the Judas tribe.

Prediction about Judas, the ancestor of Jesus:
"Judas is lion's cub, you return from the prey, my son. Like a lion, he crouches and lies down, like a lioness- who dares to rouse him? The scepter will not depart from Judas, nor ruler's staff from between his feet until Shiloh comes, and the obedience of the nations is his. (Genesis 49:9-10) As 'scepter' means a royal authority, Shiloh means the Savior, above mentioned words mean that before the Savior appears, Jesus, Judas' descendant, will rule the world all the way, but if the Savior appears, Jesus will not rule the nation.

*Prophecy for Dan
Dan will provide justice for his people as one of the tribes of Israel. Dan will be a serpent by the roadside, a viper along the path, that bites the horse' heels so that the rider tumbles backwards. I look for deliverance, Lord. (Genesis 49:16-18) The words "Dan will provide justice for his people" mean that the Savior who is the judge will come out among the offspring of

Dan.

The words "Dan will be a serpent by the roadside, a viper along the path, that bites the horse' heels so that the rider tumbles backwards." are interpreted as follows. In old times, as kings rode horses, tumbling the rider backwards means snatching a royal authority. Therefore, these words mean that the Savior from Dan tribe snatches a royal authority of Judas. So Jacob passed into Dan the authority of judgment. The words "I look for deliverance, Lord.' means that Jacob waited for salvation through Dan tribe. That is, it means that the Savior comes from the Dan tribe.

The Victor Savior on the Bible was supposed to appear among the hidden Dan people in Korea.

Prophet Isaiah said the Savior will appear not from Judas, but the Dan tribe's offspring in Korea. "Be silent before me, you islands! Who has stirred up one from the east, calling Him in righteousness to his service. He hands nations over to him and subdues kings before him. I took you from the ends of the earth, from its farthest corners I called you" (Isaiah41:1-9). Above, 'the ends of the earth, farthest corners' means Korea and Japan, God said "Be silent before me, you islands!" So Japan does not include that.

According to the second sentence, God said that he would subdue kings before the righteous man of the east. This means a king of kings is the Savior in the east. In the above words "I took you from the ends of the earth; from its farthest corners I called you.' the country, farthest corner," is only Korea. Then God sent the Dan tribe to the country where the sun rises, hid, and brought up them to stir up the Victor Savior.

* Why was Koreans called Han race(韓民族) which has the name

of God; Hananim in Korean.

Israelites called God Hananim, nowadays they call Ananim by the phenomenon of 'h' being dropped. However, today Koreans still call God Hananim. Also Korean people are called 'Han, Hana' race, also the name of nation is 'Han' country, and the Korean peninsula is 'Han' peninsula. Like this, the Koreans put one part of God's name in the name of their race, their country, and their peninsula. Nowadays nobody knows why the name of their county, their race, and their peninsula is Han. Especially, they put God in their national anthem's lyrics as follows 'because Hananim keeps and helps Korea, Korea will be forever'. Actually every country which attacked Korea was destroyed after attacking Korea. Then why do Koreans stick to God? Because Koreans are the direct descendants of God and the Savior was supposed to appear in them according to Isaiah 41:1-9 in the Bible. Therefore, God hid Dan tribe of Israel in the corner land of the Far East. Of course, there are a lot of evidences to prove that Koreans are Israelites. They are over 100 similar things between ancient Israelites and Koreans in archeology, culture, and character.

I will illustrate the similar examples using an article that I wrote in SeungRi SinMoon in 2008 after visiting Israel.

To show the similarity between Israelites and Koreans, I will cite through editing and arranging the article I put in SeungRi Sinmoon[2] of 2008, the studying on the history of Israel, Israelites, and the archeological relics.

---

[2] SeungRi Sinmoon is a biweekly newspaper, which sends messages about the advent of Neo-humans and the new words of heaven.

I went to Israel for three weeks in 2008 as a reporter by an official invitation. The aim to visit Israel was to take participate in the event of 60th anniversary of establishing Israeli government, to visit cultural and historical sites, to compare the culture of Korean and Israel, to announce the fact about the old Hebrew on the roof-tiles to Israel scholars, and to interact with archeologists of Israel. To complete my duty, I visited the National University of Hebrew and searched the Internet to the academy of archeology and the history of Hebrew to find out experts in old Hebrew. Fortunately, after many complications, I met Ed. Greenstein, a professor Bar ILan University. He told me the era of the ancient Hebrew on the roof-tiles is BC late 8~6 century.

According to Mr. Ed Greenstein, Hebrew has been changed eighteen times. He showed me the history of its change using a diagram for fifty minutes. After interviewing with him, I gave three pictures of the roof-tiles with appreciation. Ed Greenstein promised to cooperate with my academy in interacting culture. I thought that it would be impossible for old Hebrews on roof-end tiles which were found in Korea to be acknowledged by a professor of the Academy of Hebrew.

1) Similarities in genetics

Judging from the viewpoint of genetics, their appearances look alike. Their appearances and the bone of head are similar.

In the Bible, Noah had three sons, among them, Shem is the ancestor of yellow people, Japheth is the ancestor of white people, and Ham is the ancestor of Negro. Noah predicted about his three sons as follows. Ham will be the slave of Japheth; Japheth extends his territory, live in the tents of Shem. Today's white people are rich with a highly developed material civilization. Comparing with the highly developed civilization, moral civilization is as corrupt as it can go; finally, they are supposed to surrender Shem who gets ahead in moral civilization (God's civilization). It means that the Messiah appears from yellow people of Shem. Israelites were originally yellow and short with black hairs according to (Numbers 13:32~33) in the Bible. Also, Israelites are originally small like a grasshopper according to the Bible. So Korean people are still short. However, today's Israelites' blood was mixed repeatedly to survive from the targeting of Nazi and due to the occupation of the Rome. So they lost the purification of their yellow race; almost they have the appearance of white people. For example, Jesus had the appearance of the Roman such as brown hair, white complexion, and a long nose. However, Koreans still keep the purification of typical yellow race with single blood; they are short and have black hairs. Here is an article which was written in January, 1950 in one daily newspaper by one Jewish American soldier who was a doctor of anthropology. The article shows that Israelites and Koreans are the same race. The article is as follows. "I have studied the shape of cranial bones of humans according to races; I can see what races are by seeing the faces of people. Also, I can see what races' skulls are by seeing them. While I worked in Korea for 2.6 years, whenever people excavated tombs, I saw the skulls; I found that the skulls of Koreans and those of Israelites are the same."

2) Similarity in character

In character, both people have chronic bureaucratic and personal connections are considered highly. When they drive, they lose their temper easily and often use a klaxon. Their concept of time is loose; they are stubborn, conservative, and too serious. The both people are very smart and consider education highly. Therefore, although both countries are small, they are superior to other races in the world and receive the attention of the world.

3) Similarity in faith and history

As they have kept the law of God and have looked forward to the Savior through a lot of adversities. Koreans have been waiting for Jeongdoryeong, Israelites have been waiting for the Messiah. Koreans have been attacked by foreign countries around 800 times, but they survive. And Israelites were attacked a lot by foreign countries including Rome, suffered Holocaust during the First World War, wandered the world for thousands years after losing their country, and waged wars against Middle East. Through the suffering histories, the people of two countries became patriotic and strong. I was surprised to know that the year when two governments were established was 1948. Although they are separated by geographically, their fates are the same. Because the people of the two countries were chosen people by God, they were supposed to go through a lot of hardships, so they developed their strength for thousands years to change the mortal world into immortal one by producing the Savior. Therefore, the way of Israelites is a thorny path itself, which is one shedding tears of blood like the fate of the Savior.

4) Similarity in geopolitics

The two countries are very influenced now by strong countries such as America. The two countries' young men have military duty due to the division of Korea, the wars against neighboring countries and the threat of terror.

5) Similarity in the relics of ancient folk museums

After finishing the interview and participating the 60th anniversary of the establishing the government, I visited Eretz Israel museum in TelAviv on March27th. It is in 2 HaimLevanonSt., RammatAviv, its exhibits cover a wide range topics such as archeology, folklore, tradition crafts, decorative arts, cultural history and local identity. The museum also has restored production facilities including a flour mill, millstone, treadmill, watermill, a loom, a plow, smithy, and soon. It seemed like I visited the Korean folk village in Yoongin. While I stayed for more four hours to research this category in Eretz Museum in Israel, I felt that the relics of ancient Israel will be the clue to find the lost Dan clue and to reveal the hidden history of Korea.

6) Similarity in culture and living habits

Now I will enumerate similarities in culture and living habits which support that Koreans are Israelites. Koreans said sometimes 'goseule' meaning' Demons, go away' when they spread red bean soup around their houses to protect them from demons like old Israelites pasted blood on the gate-posts. Korea did not have sheep, so they used red bean soup, whose color is similar to the blood of sheep. Also in Korea, when people start their businesses or move their houses, they make rice cake with red beans and share with their neighbors to keep them from demon. Like Israelites celebrate the Passover by pasting blood on the gate-post to keep devil, Korean eat red bean soup to defeat devil on winter solstice. That is, Koreans still observe the custom the Passover of old Israelites. Additionally, they have many similar customs and cultures.

(1) Similarity in the right of the first-born

They have the custom which the oldest boys inherit a legacy from their parents.

(2) Similarity in the culture of funeral

Also they have the same funeral (burial) culture wearing hemp clothes and weeping hymn' aigo, aigo' when their family members die according to Genesis 37, 1Chronicles 21:16.

(3) Similarity in totem faith and Sodo

They built totem poles in front of the village, that is, sacred poles to keep the village from demons, to obtain abundant harvests, and to wish the health of the village people. Also They built 'Seo-nang dang', Tutelary shrine. 'Seo-nang dang' was the place where the chief gods dwelled to keep the villagers to be healthy, happy, and prosperous. The villagers performed a ritual service here at the beginning of every lunar New Year. There were Sodo areas, sacred areas, from old Chosen, the first government of Korea, to Silla era, where a chief priest performed ancestral rites to God, people in Sodo were not ruled by a king. So when even murderers or felons went to those areas, they were not arrested. I could see this example in the customs of old Israelites in Deuteronomy 19:4-6 in the Bible.

(4) Both people liked to wear hemp clothes and white ones.

In old times, old Korean women and Israel women covered their faces with cloth when they went out. Also Israelites liked wearing white clothes according to the Bible, so they were called the people of white clothes; Koreans were called the race of white clothes, too.

(5) Similarity of the system of marriage

Before marriage, the parents of bridegrooms sent silk to the houses of the bride as a present, when bridegrooms went to the house of the bride, people followed the bridegrooms carrying cheongsacholong, traditional Korean lantern with a red –and blue silk shade. And Israel and Korean bridegrooms and brides could not see each other before wedding; even they could not look at each other during a wedding ceremony. In case a bridegroom looked at the bride, people threw a pack of ash to the eyes of the bridegroom in old times.

(6) Both countries' women carried a jar of water on their heads
Women carried water in water Jars on their head from a well after chattering with neighbors on a well-side.

(7) Both countries pasted the words of God on the gate or the gateposts
　立春大吉, 建陽大慶 謹賀新年

They sometimes wrote down idiomatic phrases on the main gates, today's Koreans still do that.

(8) Both people built stone altars in front of tombs and offered ritual services, Koreans do that these days.
Both people built castles, used stone mills, and made roof-end tiles and ceramics using the same way. Also, the way to build the fortress, castle, and ondol(a system heating floors) is the same.

(9) Similarity in the ritual of religion and sacrifice
Both people have a similar religious ritual. Israelites performed a ritual offering sheep or cows on the stone altars, Koreans held rituals for rain putting calves on the stone altars; also they used the same ritual dishes or utensils.

(10) Similarity in stern notion of chastity
Both people had the stern notion of chastity. For example, old Israelites and Koreans killed women who committed adultery with throwing stones. Also both countries did not allow boys and girls to sit together after they became 7 years old. In addition, only if men and women were engaged, the women could not get married to another man.

(11) Similarity in law ancient times

They had similar laws. I could see similarity between Moses 10 commandments and the 8 Taboo laws[3] of Dan in ancient Chosen(古朝鮮: the first government of Korea). Here are old laws of Dan of the ancient Chosen.

① You, serve the only Lord.

② You, respect your parents. As your parents came from heaven, if you respect your parents, it is equal to respect heaven

③ You, women and men, get together, neither hate, nor be jealous, and nor conduct lewd.

④ You, live and help each other. Do not slander or murder each other.

⑤ You, yield each other and cultivate yourselves. You do not extort or steal.

⑥ You, do not be fierce, arrogant, or hurt things or people. Respect each other and love following the example of heaven.

⑦ You, help each other in emergency and rescue in difficulties. Do not ignore the weak people. Or you do not look down on lower people.

⑧ You, do not conceive a sly mind and do not hide an evil mind. If you respect heaven and love people, your luck is unlimited.

(12) Similarity in food

They enjoy the same food such as garlic, leather carp, spicy food, and leek.

---

[3] The Eight Taboo law, the national law of Dangun Chosen country which was built by Dangun, is the first statute law of Korea, it was written in 「Gyoowonsahwa」. It is the law that all people of old Chosen had to keep, so it is important material to study old Chosen. The copy of the eight Taboo law is exhibited in the National Central Museum, its reading number is 貴重本 629(古 2105-1).

7) Similarity in ancient Hebrew and Korean before Chinese culture

I went to America to participate in the international seminar in 2010[4]. I presented a thesis about 'the origin of Arirang in the view of the cultural history of the world and in the view of the culture of language'. While I studied the origin of Arirang, I found a surprising fact. Arirang which is sung not only Koreans but also the people of the world is originated from the faith of Israelites calling Yahweh that is the origin of Jehovah. A-Li that is the root of the words calling God is changed into Ari. Through studying about Hebrew and Sumerian language, I found that the offspring of Dan is people of Sham in ancient times; they used 'A-LA, A-LI, A-LU, A-BU', Sham's language. Therefore, I think the root of Ari is 'A-LA, A-LI' of Shem language, which were turned into A-Ri, A-RA' to pronounce easily,

Also, it is an interpretation to fit 亞(A) which is in old Korean books and funeral ritual, 百亞勝 (baekaseung) which is in prophetic books, 亞(A) is interpreted as 'Eol or Al in Korean, which means the original spirit of humans= the spirit of life= the holy spirit of God). Of course, the origin of Arirang of modern form is in「Gyeokamyourok」, the history of the root of Arirang is long. I think that Ala, the God of Muslim in the Middle East, is originated from A-Li, Shem language, which means human spirit, soul, holy spirit.

---

4) The above thesis is a part of 'Arirang Linguistic and Literary Study of the Korean Falk Song, Arirang' which I presented under the subject 'the twelfth Han Thought', in' 2010 International Conference on New Religion in Korea', on January 30, 2010, in Claremont, California, USA, co-hosted by the Process studies and the Korean Academy of New Religions. I was invited by professor, Kim Sang-Il.

So I infer that 'Li' of 'A-Li' was changed into A-Ri by the phenomenon of assonant and remained as the origin of Ari of modern Korean. There are some scholars who insist that the origin of 'A-LU' is A-La of Shem language and Assyrian language. In conclusion, I think that the origin of Arirang moved to the east by the Dan tribe that was chosen by God, in the process of the Dan tribe's moving to the Korean Peninsula, the song was made from wishing to build heaven and standing in awe of God.

Also, there is similarity between the existing ancient Korean and ancient Hebrew. For example, I think that 'ABUJI' of Korean meaning father came from' A-BI, A-BU' of Shem. The ancient language of 'ABI and AMI' of Korean meaning father and mother came from' A-BI and A-BA' and 'A-MI and U-MA' of ancient Hebrew. AN and ANU meaning God has the similar meaning of ANA and ANI of Shem language, they are interpreted as 'Han' in Mongol, China, and Korea.

There is famous HAPOALIM BANK in Israel. It is pronounced as APOALIM, but they write 'HAPOALIM' in the way of ancient Hebrew. Like that, Dan tribe came to the east having the habit of ancient language culture, so they write HANANIM and HANUNIM meaning God. However, there are few scholars who know that the root that Korea is called Han country came from ancient Hebrew. Judging from the culture of language, Korean is surely the people of God. Furthermore, the root of 'HANU, HANA,' is God. Then what is the essence of God? There is HANUKA, the holiday of light, in Israel. The root of 'HANU=ANU' in HANUKA symbolizes God, so I could certainly see that from the meaning of 'HANUKA', "the essence of God is light" and it coincides with the definition of God of the Bible. Therefore, 「Gyeokamyourok」 predicted in the part of Hein that Jeongdoryeong would come as ARI (亞理), the hero of Ariryeong would appear with the Sweet Dew. 'The Sweet Dew is the Holy Dew Spirit, according to Hosea 14:5, it is the symbol of the Victor, the brilliant light of the Reincarnate Maitreya Buddha according to Nirvana Sutra. Therefore, the existence that comes as light is Ariryeong Jeongdoryeong, who all humans have been waiting for. So judging from the abovementioned similarity between two country, Koreans who have inherited the traditional of ancient Israel is the offspring of Dan, the fifth son of Jacob, who received the right of the first-born from Jacob, moved to the east, settled in the Korean Peninsula, and produced the Victor Savior. Here is an article by the former ambassador of Israel, who worked in Korea 8 years. He admitted that Koreans were ancient Israelites. The article of August 1st, 2005 in Choseonilbo, a daily newspaper of Korea. The corner of the newspaper is 'I look into the world in Korea' By Ujimanor, Israeli ambassador, who will leave on August 7th. The title was "Koreans and Israelites were the same race in ancient times.

I could not find the feeling of farewell on the face of Israeli ambassador who will leave Korea on August 7th. When a reporter of Chosenilbo went to the embassy of Israel and opened his mouth, the ambassador waved his hand. " When he came to Korea in1970 for the first time, he worked as a consul for 4 years, this time I have worked for 4 years as an ambassador. When I left Korea in August, 1974, I said to my wife that staying Korea was too good, someday, I will come back here. 27 years later, I volunteered as Israel ambassador to Korea, I came to Seoul in September, 2001." However, that is not first his tie with Korea. His connection with Korea traces back to more. "In graduate school, I studied international relationship, my major was Northeast Asia." At that time the ambassador heard that Korea is very similar to Israel "Ancient Israel was composed of

12 tribes. The country was attacked by a foreign country and collapsed. The Israelites scattered to Europe, Asia, Africa, and so on. Among 12 tribes, only one tribe's whereabouts remains a mystery. The lost tribe's family name is Dan. The founder of old Chosen is Dangun. It is interesting." He is the first mania of Hallyu; He enjoyed the songs of Boa, a Korean singer, Pansori; a Korean traditional music, he likes Korean traditional food. But whenever he has chances to go singing rooms, he sings Hebrew songs. They are Habanaguila meaning let's be happy. The lost tribe's family name is Dan, the founder of Korea is Dan gun. Both people are warm hearted.

"What would you like to say to Koreans?", then he asked, "Do you know Sabra? He continued." It means native of Israel. Originally, Sabra is a kind of cactus. Its surface is hard with thorns. But its fruit is very sweet. The Israelites are the same. Because of the exterior circumstance, they seems to be difficult to treat, however, they are very kind and warm." Then he gave the reporter a bottle of alcohol that is made from Sabra. When the reporter came back home and drank it, the fragrance of chocolate and orange filled his mouth. The article is finished with "I can see what the ambassador wanted to say finally." [5]

4.The New Interpretations of by the Victor

Through the words of the Victor, I hope that the readers learn how to interpret the Bible. As the God who told in the Bible is in the Victor, he knows the Bible exactly. I will introduce the words of the Victor.

Thus Have I Heard on Feb 4th, 1990 from the Savior. (In these 'words, This man indicates the Victor).

---

[5] By Jeon Byeon Geun, a reporter of Choseonilbo (blog) bkjeon. chosun. Com.

What is religion? What does the Bible talk about? Does spirit leave the body after death? Does heaven really exist? If heaven exists, where is it? Also if hell exits, we should know where it is. Why do people die? According to the Bible, people die due to the wages of sin, how does sin kill people? We should know it in detail. The Bible says that people are saved due to faith, and then what is faith? Is faith in the Bible a believing mind or other existence? When we know the answer of the abovementioned questions, we can believe what the Bible says. The Bible and the Buddhist scriptures have similar words or the same ones a lot. Therefore, there are the same words and meaning in the Bible and the Buddhist scriptures. So if people live as the Bible says, they live as the Buddhist scriptures say, if people live as the Buddhist scriptures say, they live as the Bible says.

The Bible writes that Adam and Eve died due to eating the forbidden fruit, and their descendants have died because of it. However, nobody showed the forbidden fruit. Nobody taught it. If nobody teaches people it, it means that nobody knows the Bible. The Bible says if people eat the fruit of life, they live forever. However, were there men who gave the fruit of life? Is there any man who can explain the fruit of life? If nobody explains it, it means that nobody knows the Bible. So, today, we can see easily by asking about the fruit of life whether there are religions or not, which people believe as the Bible says. If people do not teach definitely the fruit of life, their religion is led as the Bible says. Also if people do not teach definitely the forbidden fruit, their religion is not one by the Bible, either. Therefore, the only man who knows the Bible can teach definitely people where heaven is, where hell is, whether Satan fly or not, what Satan looks like, what Satan is, and who God is. So that is for the man who knows God and the truth. Although a religionist does not know about the words, if he asks his followers to believe the religion without questions, the religionist is a fake. Hence, people say that they believe their religions as the Bible or the Buddhist scriptures say, but they do not know the meaning of 'people die due to the wage of sin' though the Bible and the Buddhist scriptures say it. Therefore, today if people say that a wrong behavior is sin, it is a worldly interpretation. If people commit sins in the world, they go to prisons. The words "if people have bad behavior, it is sin, and if they have good behavior, it is not sin," are worldly ones. So people are able to study and to know the truth by knowing righteousness and sin definitely. Therefore, did This man say that there were religions that people believed as the Bible says? There are no religions that people believe as the Bible tells. Although the Bible says that to recover the Garden of Eden is the will of God. However, in fact, they do not know how the Garden of Eden will be completed, what the Garden of Eden is like, where the Garden of Eden is built, who will build it. They do not even know whether God builds the Garden of Eden or humans build it. Are there are religions that people believe as the Bible says. No, all religions are false. The Bible records that people are saved due to faith. Although they do not know it, they say about faith. So listen to This man's theory of faith, the theory of salvation, and the theory of the Savior. This man speaks in detail about the fruit of life, which is the manna of life. First, This man will speak of the theory of faith. Faith is, as it is now, a gift that God gives according to Ephesians 2:8, all pastors of Christianity say like that. In fact they do not know its meaning. They say without knowing its true meaning. They just say because the Bible says so. Since they do not know it, they cannot say about the definition. Therefore, as it is now, faith is the Gift that God gives.

Faith is the essence of God and is the evidence of what they could not see according to Hebrew. So if everything is accomplished as they wished, they can see what they could not see, they can see the heaven they could not see, they can see God who they could not see, and they can see angels. So when people can see all things which they could not see, that is the evidence of faith. To see is faith. Faith comes from knowing. If people do not know, they cannot believe. Therefore, if pastors tell their followers to believe without questions, it cannot be faith. So although people have mustard seed-sized faith, if they order this mountain to move there, the mountain will be moved. It is faith according to the Bible. Therefore, it means that faith has power. Is the above mentioned 'this mountain' worldly? It is a spiritual mountain because the words of the Bible are spiritual. As it is now, does a Spiritual Mountain indicate mind or body? It is mind. So the words 'this mountain is moved' are removing a sinful mind. Therefore, the faith that This man speaks about is Biblical, not the worldly faith which people know. This man speaks about faith to tell the theory of salvation. The Bible writes that people are saved due to faith. After Jesus appeared, did faith come to exist? Before Jesus appeared, there was faith that people believed in God. Therefore, as it is now, Jesus said, "the king of the world would come after me" according to John 14:30. Therefore, as it is now, Jesus confessed that he is not the king of the world. Should we believe the Bible except those words? We should believe the Bible wholly. The Isaiah 34:16, in the Bible, it says," Look at the scroll of the Lord and read: None of these will be missing, not one will lack her mate. For it is his mouth that has given the order, and his Spirit will gather them together" . It means that all God's words have their mate. If the words of the Bible do not have their mate, they are not God's words, that is, they are those of Satan. None of the words of God lack a mate. Every word of the Bible does not its mate. Hence, in Genesis, in the Bible, it writes that people can live forever by eating the fruit of life. Then the Bible says that the words of the Bible are spiritual. The fruit of life is the words of spirit, it is the fruit of spirit, and spirit is mind. Therefore, an immortal mind is the fruit of life. So the words of the Bible have their mate. Therefore, the words that people do not die by eating the fruit of life means that because the fruit of life is spiritual words, the fruit of life is spiritual fruit, spiritual fruit is spirit, the spirit is one which gives eternal life, which overcomes death, conscious awareness of 'I'. The spirit which defeats conscious awareness of 'I' is the fruit of life. Like this, the man who teaches definitely the fruit of life is the man who teaches the Bible. Pouring oil teaches the Bible. As it is now, people cannot learn the Bible in theology colleges. Therefore, as it is now, people can learn the Bible by pouring oil. Therefore, as it is now, the abovementioned oil is sesame oil? No, it is not. It is the oil of spirit. Therefore, as is now, today the Bible records that pouring oil teaches the Bible, the oil is not sesame oil, but the oil of the Holy Spirit. Only the Spirit of God knows the Bible. Therefore, today, This man can teach the Bible 66's volumes for an hour and interpret it easily, because God accompanies This man. Yesterday, there was a lecture about the advent of Jeongdoryeong in Busan. Around 800–900 people including the followers of the Victory Altar attended the lecture. Among them, 100 new comers came to Busan Victory Altar. Now, it is almost the time when many people will crowd here. This man said last year that new comers would crowd the next year. They are supposed to come. People can live forever by eating the fruit of life. This man says each time that the fruit of life is the Spirit of God that overcomes self-consciousness of 'I', Satan, and death. The mind of God that overcomes self-consciousness of 'I' (Satan) is the fruit of life. Therefore, people go to heaven by accomplishing immortality. The Bible writes, "nor will people say, 'Here it is,' or 'There it is,' because the kingdom of God is within you."

Also the Bible says where God dwells, heaven is. Only God goes to heaven. People cannot go to heaven. This man just teaches the Bible not the study of humans. This man does not try to humor people. The Bible tells that only God goes to heaven, because heaven is the house of God. So people can go to heaven by becoming God. And the Bible says that you can be saved by being reborn as the Spirit of God. Being reborn as the Spirit of God means that people should be reborn as the Spirit of God to live forever. If people are reborn as God, are they humans? No, they are n't. If people are reborn as God, they are God. Please read the Bible in detail. Foolish people are blinded by the words "just believe without question and think that they will go to heaven if they believe the Bible without question." That's absurd. In the world people believe when they have faith. Do you lend money to a passerby? If you do not believe him, you do not lend money. As the words are worldly ones, they are different from the meaning of the faith of the Bible. Faith is believed by knowing. If people do not know something, they cannot believe it. When people know the whereabouts of the heaven, they believe that they go to heaven. People will believe in heaven when they are taught exactly where it is and what heaven is like. As it is now, people believe eternal life when they know the secret of immortality. If they force people to believe in immortality without logical explaining it, will they believe immortality? No, they will not. So people believe in immortality by knowing its way. Those who say that they believe the words of the Bible without questions, tell a lie. So as it is now, the words "people are saved by being reborn as the Holy Spirit" mean that they get salvation by being reborn as God. The words "people get salvation by being reborn as God" mean that "people were God before they became humans." The words "humans were God" are hidden in the words "people are saved by being reborn as the Holy Spirit." Humans were God; the God was captivated in the prison of Satan and became the slave of Satan. If people kill Satan, consciousness of 'I', they can be reborn as the Holy Spirit. Also the Bible says that people are saved by being revived. By being revived, humans can be saved and live forever according to the Bible. Revival itself is the word of the Bible. Therefore, the word 'revival' is the word of the Bible, its meaning is living again. The words "all dead bodies will be revived from their tombs" are ones of crazy men. The words of revival of the Bible means to live again from tombs, the tombs are spiritual tombs. Revival is spiritual revival, too. It means to spiritually live again. The Bible should be taught like this. Does Christianity teach like this? If it cannot teach like this, it is a false religion. Therefore, the words that people are saved by being revived are that people should be revived from their spiritual tombs. It means that God who is captured in a spiritual tomb breaks it. Also the words "people are saved by being revived "mean living again from a tomb, which means that God who is in a spiritual tomb breaks the spiritual tomb, kills Satan, and revives from the prison of Satan. That is resurrection. You should teach pastors the meaning of resurrection because they are unaware. So the words "people are saved by being revived" mean to live again. To live again means that, because the Bible is about God, God in a spiritual tomb overcomes consciousness of 'I' (Satan and death). The spiritual tomb which is Satan is just consciousness of 'I'. That is, because Satan is consciousness of 'I', which is sin. So in James 1:15, in the Bible, it says, "after desire has conceived, it gives birth to sin, and sin, when it is full-grown, gives birth to death. So desire is sin. Desire itself does not attempt desire, 'I' attempt desire. Viewed in the words that people can see the tree by its fruit, because the tree of consciousness of 'I' bares desire, if desire is sin, consciousness of 'I' is sin and Satan. Consciousness of 'I' is Satan, sin, and the forbidden fruit according to the Bible. However, nobody teaches it. Therefore, due to sin, as it is now, people die. Are there the men who teach definitely 'sin'? Because desire is sin, if people attempt desire, their blood decays. When people eat food attempting desire, they have stomachache, so if they get acupunctured, black blood oozes. The reason is because at the moment people attempt desire, their blood decays. So, as it is now, due to blood's decaying, germs are made in the decayed blood, people catch serious diseases, and they finally die.

Therefore, people become old and die because their blood decays. Therefore, due to desire, the blood of people decays, and they die. The words of the Bible "desire is sin" are right. It is scientifically right. Does desire itself attempt desire or do 'I' attempt desire? I attempt desire. Because the conscious awareness of 'I' attempt desire, it is the original sin and Satan, so it is the forbidden fruit. Therefore, the words "due to the forbidden fruit, people were destined to die" mean that due to having the mind of Satan, people die. Hence, the words "to throw away 'I' all the time" in the Bible and the Buddhist scriptures mean not to eat the forbidden fruit, but to vomit it. Also the words "if people eat the fruit of life, they live forever' mean, when they eat the Spirit of God, the conqueror of Satan, and the Spirit of

God becomes their consciousness, people do not die. Although there are words 'if people eat the Spirit of God that overcomes the ego, Satan, death, and they can live forever in the Bible'. Nobody explained it until now. Unless people explain it, they cannot be the men who teach the Bible. The words 'due to eating the forbidden fruit, people were destined to die' mean that people die by eating the spirit of Satan(consciousness of T). The consciousness of T is the forbidden fruit, Satan, and a spiritual tomb according to the Bible. So today, consciousness of T is a tomb, when people kill the consciousness of T and throw it away, the Spirit of God that is locked in the prison of Satan becomes people's consciousness, and they live again. This is resurrection. Being reborn as the Holy Spirit means being revived. People are saved by being revived; also they are saved by being reborn as the Holy Spirit in the Bible. All the words of the Lord have a mate. Having a mate means having the same meaning. So the words 'people are saved by being reborn as the Holy Spirit, the word 'people are saved by eating the fruit of life,' the words 'people are saved by being revived,' and the words 'a martyr is saved' have the same meaning. The word 'martyr' is the word of the Bible. The Bible says that a martyr is the man who dies for God. That is, martyr is a man who throws away his / her life for God. However, the words of the Bible themselves are spiritual. Martyrdom is a spiritual one. Therefore, spiritual martyrdom is the word of the mind. Hence spiritual martyrdom means that my mind dies for God, God sits at the place of my mind. So when the Spirit of God becomes T , I will be revived as God and become a martyr. They should teach definitely the Bible like this. Do the men who graduated from theological colleges have a qualification to teach the Bible? So today, as it is now, a martyr is a resurrected man. A resurrected man is a man reborn as the Holy Spirit. The man who is reborn as Holy Spirit is the man who eats the fruit of life. The man who eats the fruit of life is the man who eats the Spirit of God and the mind of God, which will overcome Satan and death. Therefore, the man who eats the fruit of life indicates one who is reborn as the Holy Spirit, is resurrected, and becomes a martyr. This man taught the words of 90 percent of the Bible (66books) by saying this much. The Bible says that the Garden of Eden is recovered; it is the house of God and heaven. Also, the Bible says, "Neither shall they say, here or there, for, behold, the kingdom of God is within you according Nuke 17:21. And the Bible says where God dwells, heaven is. Do people go to heaven after they die? If people die, do they have their minds? When people die, their spirit die, their lives die and bodies die, too. Does the life of people exist separately from a body? Because life is in a body, spirit is in a body, as it is now, spirit is blood, and a body is formed by blood, and spirit and life exists in a body. So the words "when people die, their spirit leaves their bodies" are illogical words. If religionists tell incorrect facts, then their religions are false. If the history of a religion is long, is it a true religion? No, it is not. No matter how long history a religion has, false religion cannot be true. No matter how long a man lives as a blind man, he is a blind man. No matter how long a fool lives, he is still a fool. Therefore, as it is now, today, there are words "if people know the way of eternal life, they cannot die." Although the words are worldly, it is a truth. People can escape death by knowing the immortal way. People can go to heaven by knowing the way. Knowing is faith. So the source of wisdom is God according to Proverb. Faith is God, who destroys the ego, Satan, and death. So the Spirit of God who overcomes consciousness 'I', Satan, and death is not only faith but also the fruit of life because the Spirit of God overcomes the ego, Satan, and death. It can be free from the prison of Satan. The resurrected man is God who overcomes his ego, Satan, and death. Being resurrected means living again. Living again means that people can live by overcoming death. This man pairs the words of the Bible. The words of This man are always the same as what you listened to through a video of 8 years ago. Is that because This man smart? Because the Spirit of God in This man tells the truth. As only the Spirit of God says about the words of God, the truth, He always tells the same. Therefore, today, salvation is accomplished by becoming God, who can live forever by God destroying the ego, Satan, and death. Therefore, wherever God who defeats his ego, Satan, and death goes, heaven is. Does the Bible say that heaven is in the sky or in the mind of men? It says that heaven is in men. So, as it is now, the Garden of Eden is in the mind of the Victor, the conqueror of the ego. Therefore, the will of Bible was accomplished. People can learn the words of the Bible and all the truth in the world are accomplished by the will of the Bible. Unless the will of God is realized, the Consummator cannot appear. When God is completed, He is supposed to know and say the secret of Satan, the secret of killing Satan, as it is now, and teach the weapons of killing Satan. Due to the teaching of killing Satan by the Victor, all people can become Victors and be reborn as the Holy Spirit. Then all of them become Victors (Savior), resurrected existence, and martyrs. Therefore, when the Bible writes about the Savior, does the Bible say that the Savior will appear in Europe? No, it does n't. It says that the Savior will turn up in the East. "Keep silent before me, O islands, I will raise up the righteous man from the east, make him rule over kings", according to Isaiah 41:1-9. Therefore, because the Bible says, "Keep silent, island," the Lord will raise up the righteous man in the East, Japan is excluded. From the old times, the countries of the East are Korea and Japan. The Bible says that I will take you from the ends of the earth; it means that God will call the righteous man from the land of corner, among the countries of the East. Also the Bible says that God will make him rule over kings. So the righteous man is the king of kings. Jesus said in John 14:30 that the ruler of the world is coming after me." The ruler is coming from not Europe but Korea according to the prophecy of prophet, Isaiah. Isaiah said about the place of the advent of the Savior. Genesis 49:16 says about the race of the Savior. It says that Jacob gave Dan jurisdiction among 12 sons. Jacob predicted for his 12 sons, the prediction for Judas is that you are a lion's cub, Judah, the scepter will not depart from Judas, until Shiloh (the Savior) comes. The prediction "Judah is a lion's cub" is that he is a man who kills humans. That is, he is Satan. "Dan shall judge his people; he shall be a serpent by the roadside, a viper along the path, which bites the horse heels, so that the horse rider shall fall backward. I look for your deliverance, Lord." Those words mean that the Savior comes from Dan tribe. The words' throwing the horse rider to the ground' mean killing the false Savior, because only kings rode horses in the olden times, throwing the rider means killing the false Savior, the king of Satan's world. If the jurisdiction went to Dan, the God of Jacob went to Dan. Please read Genesis 49:16, it says that Dan will judge his people. Only God judges people. Isaiah 41 says the God of beginning is the righteous man of the east, the God of omega. Therefore, we can see that the judge God came to Dan in Genesis 49:16. So because God came to the Dan tribe, they are blessed as chosen people. The Bible writes that Dan tribe was lost to the northeast 3000 years ago. Nobody knows where Dan tribe moved. The Koreans' grandfather is Dan Gun. Gun is not a name but respectful suffix; its meaning is a king. His original name is Dan. His descendants called him like that. Dan's grandfather is the fifth son of Jacob, his mother is Rachel, who is the first wife of Jacob according to the Bible. Isaac, the first son of the first wife of Abraham inherited from his father. In view of what has taken place that Isaac, the first son of the first wife of Abraham inherited the right of the first-born. People can see that Jacob passed Dan, the eldest son of the first wife of Jacob, the right of the first- born in Genesis 49:16. So after God accompanied Dan tribe, they came to Korea. The tribe of Dan moved to the east from Zora of Israel 3000 years ago, passing Syria, Iraqi, and Iran, crossing the seas, passing through broad China, living the Altai for 100 years, passing Manchuria, crossing the Abrok River, and founding old Chosen by the Daedong River. Therefore, the roof-tiles that were founded by the riverbank of the Daedong River were round shape, have Hebrew on them. So that is the evidence that the ancestors of Koreans used Hebrew. It tells that Koreans are Israelites. Also, the culture of Koreans says that they are Israelites. Further, a Korean encyclopedia writes that the head bone of Koreans is the same as that of Israelites. That is an enough evidence to identify that Koreans are Israelites. Besides, Israelites liked to wear white clothes according to the Bible, Koreans liked to wear white clothes. That is a traditional habit. So Koreans are called the people of white clothes. Also the Bible writes that old Israelites wore hemp clothes and made sound when their family member died. They built a stone altar when they performed ancestral rites according to the lyrics of a hymn. 'Like Jacob woke up and built a stone altar, we hope to awake, pray all the time, and build altars.' The people who build stone altars in front of the tombs are only Koreans, the pure race of Israelites. Although Christianity sings the hymn, they do not know that Koreans are Israelites because they are false. Therefore, the Savior was supposed to come from Korea because the God of Jacob came to Dan tribe, there is a promise that the Judge Savior will appear from the root of Dan tribe. So This man says that the Savior appears from the tribe of Dan. However, the Koreans do not know that Koreans are Israelites. They think that the father of Dan Gun came down from heaven and married a bear; Dan Gun was born from them. No matter how advanced genetic engineering becomes, a dog begets puppies, a dog cannot bear a human. Has a bear ever given birth to a human? There are a lot of foolish scholars such as evolutionists who think that monkeys have evolved from ameba, humans have evolved from monkeys. Today, humans are the children of God according to the Bible, at that moment God was captivated by Satan, God was turned into humans. Humans haven't evolved from monkeys. Also This man tells scientifically that humans cannot be born from bears. The Savior appears from the Dan tribe in Korea leads a new culture to make humanity God. Now I will introduce the new culture of neohumans.

5. The New Culture by Neohumans & The Final Issue of NRMs
The New Culture by Neohumans
We need to think that how we should live to keep up with in the new era. Because people's value determines their life environment, behaviors, character building, and even their faces. It is the time when we should rethink of the true philosophy, the true religion, and a wise life for humanity's happiness beyond existing imperfect philosophies and religions. Also now is the

time when we examine the aim of humanity's existence and the essence of humanity. As when a president is changed, the policy of the country and the social order are changed, the killing culture that was created by ignorance and death will be changed. What will be changed in the new era? What cultural structure will be formed? That is one of themes which scholars of the world new religions, philosophers, and futurists eye on. Speaking briefly, I'll say only the key point. There are two kinds of culture. One is that of saving life, the other is that of killing life. The culture in a new era is that of saving life. The culture to kill and decay life will disappear due to the advent of neohumans. The culture of saving life and the culture of salvation will be mainstream. A culture to kill life is one to kill life by decaying blood, making humanity lose vitality, and leading them to tombs. I think a new culture will bring about a large reform of the society in politic, economic, social, and cultural aspect.

1) In the aspect of politics, the era will introduce the system of politics that will be governed by the judge who teaches the proverbs. People of heaven will rule the era by the advice and helping of neohumans, the political culture of unity of the church and state will be formed.

2) In the aspect of economics, there will be no the difference between the rich and the poor. They will regard everybody as my body, so nobody dies of hunger. Also the system of economic will be changed into the system of one family. By developing a sea route and an air route and information technology device, circulation physical distribution will be fast. So through demanding forecasting, supply without waste will make a new era affluent economically.

3) In the aspect of society, the discrimination of status will disappear; will be changed to regard everyone as my body step by step. Also, in the era, people will not get married due to the view of Samsedeungmyeong after life, the philosophy of immortality, and the wisdom of heaven. The era will become an honest and righteous society, they will respect each other and practice the public philosophy.

4) In the aspect of the culture, like the prediction of Jeremiah16, the culture that people get married and have children will disappear. Also the culture of funeral will disappear, too. Here are some cultural aspects of the future.
(1) The high developed engineering of life and the culture of saving life will be formed.
(2) An era of light, unlimited life-span era will come soon.
(3) People will live as a single and try to be completed as their original essence, God.
(4) Welfare and welfare facilities will expand.
(5) Neohumans who will live as their conscience will become more.
(6) The community of the earth will be formed to save lives.
(7) Neohumans who experience the food of heaven and eat it every day will reach the level to live without eating and sleeping, will lead the era of eternal life. That is, in the ear, people can live on the fruit of life, the Holy Dew Spirit.
(8) Welcoming the era of the Big Change and the era of bright light, people will be reborn as neohumans and fly as they want. Their flying speed will be faster than the sunlight. Because, the era has neither time nor space, only if they think of something, it will be done in a moment as they want. The necessities to form

such a future society are the hidden manna, the authority of the Victor, and the secret of immortality. If people do not know all three things, they cannot accomplish immortality. That is a key point of the prophetic books. Abovementioned the prediction of the future culture will be accomplished when people try to understand the culture of neohumans, practice it, and when they listen to the message of heaven and practice it, according to Gyeoamyourok. The prophetic book suggests an assignment about how people should live and also give an answer to people. In that respect, the book is greater than any other prophetic books. There is a recording, "there will spread a mystery disease all around. It is so terrible that if people catch the disease in the morning, they die in the evening." "If people do not practice the Law of Liberty and the words of the Victor, the Victor will not keep people from the disease." in Gyeoamyourok. Of course it has a way of overcoming the disease. The predictions are the same as those of other scriptures of Korean new religions.

6. The Final Issue of NRMs

The final issue of NRMs is the salvation through physical immortality. Humanity should know the hidden manna to live forever. Also, the culture of eternal life and the way of being reborn as the Holy spirit should be revealed as soon as possible to all humanity because if there are many people who are reborn as the Holy Spirit, the immortal world will be built more quickly. God promised in all the scriptures that he would build the immortal world.

1) The Culture of Immortality

John5:39 records, "You diligently study the Scriptures because you think that by them you possess eternal life."
Titus 1:2, "a faith and knowledge resting on the hope of eternal

life, which God, who does not lie, promised before the beginning of time." John2:25, "this is what he promised us even eternal life." Like that God promised eternal life and he came to the world to keep his promise. So the aim of religion is to realize physical immortality, only God has a qualification to lead religion. Therefore, there was no religion so far.

2)The Hidden Manna, the Fruit of Life
The Bible records the hidden manna, the Victor. The symbol of the Victor is the hidden manna. This is the issue of the world.

3)The Hidden Victor in the Bible
The Victor was predicted secretly. So we should know 'when', 'where', and 'who' builds the paradise. That also can become a final issue.

Closing

Not only NRMs of Korea but also all the world new religions have the same aim, that is to build heaven. However, they do not know the concrete way and contents about it. Because the work of humanity's religion was led by the ignorant and dark spirit, not by God. Also religion and philosophies suggested the way of humanity' life not the way of going to heaven(becoming God). So they have wandered without seeing the light of God. Although originally humanity was God, they are the offspring of God who received the blood of Adam and Eve's blood, they are conscious of neighbors as enemies, have lived a ignorant life fighting. Humanity who did not know the essence of God have lived as the slaves of splitting Satan killing the lives of humanity, did know that their killing lives means killing God. So they lived as crazy men waging the Holy wars or the crusaders without knowing the meaning and aims of religions. That history of ignorant and dark death shows evidence that the spirit of death has ruled the world and become the owners of humanity. Now, all humanity will welcome a new era by the Victor of the east and the new culture of neohumans according to the Victor of the Victory Altar.

I think that the building of the paradise relies on how many neohumans are produced in the Victory Altar and how fast awaken neohumans form the culture of neohumans and understand and learn it by experience. Now, we should dump the religions, philosophies, faith and science by humanity; overcome the wave of death through the conviction of immortality, and think of the advent of the Victor who recovers the paradise. As the door of salvation is opened, the hope of immortality is in front of us. It will be a new paradigm which will lead the world new new religious movement. Due to it, the wave of eternal life will flow strongly through all humanity's heart. That is my anticipation as the result of my studying NRMs of Korea. In the Bible, Corinthians15: 26 and 15: 53 record, "the last thing to be destroyed is death". "When the perishable has been clothed with the imperishable, and the mortal with immortality, then the saying that is written will come true: "Death has been swallowed up in victory." Those are the predictions of eternal life, before the Victor comes, they had to be hidden, and nobody solved them.

The hidden manna in the Bible is the symbol and the possess condition of the Victor, the Maitreya Buddha, is the most important factor that determines the true Savior according to all the scriptures that were recorded by receiving wisdom of the Holy Spirit. Choi Je Woo angel predicted 100 years later, the advent of nonpolar eternal life, the era of immoral neohumans(

新人間) who would eat the medicine of God(仙藥), the food of heaven. The next angel of fire luck, Gang Jeung San foretold in chapter 81 of「Junghwa scripture」, his book, if the dharma rain (法雨)of the Sweet Dew(甘露)falls, it will save humanity. Also, Pak Tae Sun, the angel of wood luck predicted in the Faith paper 「信仰新報」, 1135 ho on Dec 7th, 1981, that the man who pours down the Holy Dew Spirit is the olive tree, in the same paper, 1195 ho, April 18th, 1983, "The man will fill the number of neo-human. When the number is filled, the condition of the building of the paradise will be changed." Mr. Cho Hee Sung, the angel of gold luck, preached on Jan 11th, 2002, "As the hidden manna is the fruit of life, the spirit of the Victorious God, one can eat the fruit of life by receiving the Holy Dew Spirit from the face, eyes, and body of the Victor, and then he/she defeats himself/herself, and becomes God.

If the Victor is not charged of the sins of followers, a lot of people will die. Soon, people will be able to see that the prophet like Mosses is the Victor, the truth, the way of right life, and the door of salvation." The Holy Dew Spirit is the spirit of the Victorious God that defeated the spirit of death, Satan. Therefore, ordinary people cannot see the spirit with their naked eye, but it is taken by cameras, the Victory Altar gives everybody chances to take pictures. However righteous men whose sin was washed away can see the phenomenon that God descends. That is a big hope and blessing to today's people. So Corinthians 13:10 predicted, "when perfection comes, the imperfect disappears" in the Bible. Also Revelations predicted that today, the righteous man of the east, the Victor, and white people, neo-humans, would appear. Isaiah recorded thousands years ago that the work of the Holy Spirit would be done in Korea. Let me introduce the predictions of Gyeokamyourok, the Bible, the Victor of the Bible synthetically. Those who do not join in the work of heaven by the Victor Savior who recovered His almighty or consider the work as others' work and do not cooperate with God will fall behind, collapse, or have the dark future. That is the common predictions. Further, although the Savior came to the world wearing a body of humanity in Korea and has done the work of revolution changing the mortal world into an immortal one for 33years, pouring the hidden manna, if humanity does not participate at the building of the paradise, or not listen to the words of neohumans, the future of humanity will not exist.

That is, according to 「Gyeokamyourok」, if humanity loses the Savior, they will miss the Savior who will prevent humanity from the state of crisis, disasters and mysterious diseases, will not avoid them. Also it recorded if the Savior emits the Sweet Dew, the incomplete philosophies, science and religions will lose their light and perish at the same time. Reflecting the prediction, I have a feeling if the culture of neohumans spreads to the world, the phenomenon will happen from that time. The assignment is to learn the way of being reborn as the Holy Spirit, eating the fruit of life, the way of immortality through the words of the Victor. The Victor preached if humanity regards everyone as my body and practice the philosophy, they will become neohumans. The most valuable thing to humanity is being reborn as the Victorious God. To do that, one should listen to the words of the Savior and learn the culture of neohumans. Like a title of my book, the final issue of the world new religions is getting out of the stream of death.

The man who removes death is the true Savior. The final new religious movement by the Holy Spirit in Korea is progressed as the will of God and the predictions of all the scriptures of the world. By neohumans being fostered, the basis of the paradise is built. As the predictions of Hosea 14:5, Isaiah 26:19 were accomplished, death will disappear soon, and the era of immortality will come. To establish the era soon, we should hurry to study how all humanity eat the hidden manna. The Bible and Gyeokamyourok record when light comes out from the Savior, all humanity come to the area from Incheon to Bucheon in Korea where the Savior stays. This unprecedented issue will open a new era of saving life.

I hope that my thesis will be a guide book in order for all humanity to find the way of an everlasting happiness and life. Also, I hope the scholars of the world new religions use my paper in researching the starting point and the last aim of NRMs of Korea, the Victor of the Bible, the religious revolution of the Victory Altar.

Conference

1. Books

高藤聰一郎 著, 「仙-不老不死」 translated by Choi WoonGwon, (Seoul: Boseong publisher, 1985).

Deepak Chopra, 「Men do not grow old」 translated by Lee Gyoo-Hyeong (Seoul: Jeongsin Segyesa, 1993)

Jewish Publication Society, 「JPS Hebrew-English」, Tanakh, (Philadelphia, 1999)

John. F. Walvoord, 「Major Bible Prophecies」 Zondervan Publishing House, (Michigan, 1991)

Kim Seong Suk, 「The Law of Liberty volume 1」, (Seoul: Doseo Publishing Haein, 1992).

Kim Jong Seo, 「Koreans, the children of God」, supplements, (Seoul: Institute of the science of Hanguk, 2008).

Kim Jong Man, 「Biography of Jeongdoryeong」, (Seoul: Doseo Publishing Haein, 1993).

Kwon Hee-Soon, 「THE SCIENCE OF IMMORTALITY」, (Seoul: Publishing HAE-IN, 1993)

Michael Baigent, Richard Leigh, Heny Lincoln, 「Holy blood Holy Grail」, Dell Book, New York, 1983

Park YoungJin, 「The Victory Altar where eternal life is accomplished」, (Bucheon: Doseo Publishing Haein, 2001).

徐輔睦, 「The thought of Jeongdoryeong」, (Seoul: Doseo Publishing Haein, 1996).

The Academy of the Victory Altar, 「The theory of immortality」, (Seoul: Doseo Publishing Haein, 1990).

Lee YoungJu, 「New discovery and creation」, (Seoul: Doseo Publishing Haein, 1989).

Lee SangHo(李祥昊), 「大巡典經」, (Jeonju: the headquarter of Jeungsan, 1979).

Underwood, L. H. 「Underwood of Korea」, (New York, Fleming H. Revell company, 1918).

Tak Myeong Hwan, 「New religion of Korea」Christianity Volume 4, the Institute

of the Problem of Korean Religion, (Seoul: Gukjong Publisher, 1987).
"Sinai" Publishing, 「The Holy Scriptures」, (Tel aviv, Israel, 1977)
Han Sang Yeong,「the science of immortality1」,(Seoul: Doseo Publishing Haein, 1987).
Heo Yeong Man, 「ggol1」, People can see a reflection of a person's mind by looking at the face (Goyang city: Wisdom House, 2008).

2. Dissertations
Kim Jong Seok, 「the faith of immortal body of immortality of the Victory Altar」 a doctoral dissertation,(Cheonan: Sun Moon University graduate school, 2009).
Yoon Taek Lim, 「The Methodology for Qualitative Study of the Culture and History」, (Seoul: Doseo Publishing Arce, 2004).
Han Gang-Hyen, The study of prediction of 「Gyeokamyourok」 (the culture of Korean prediction and the Victory Altar), a master's thesis(Tokyo: Mejiro University Graduate School, 2002).

3. Newspapers
<<Sports Chosun>> 1992. 9. 19
<< Chosun Ilbo>> 1992. 9. 24
<<Hanguk Ilbo>> 1993. 1. 25
<<Seoul Business Newspaper>> 1993. 2. 19

4. Books of hidden secret
「Gyeokamyourok」, which National Jungang Library has, the number of the list of old books: 1496-4 호.
佛法秘傳書,「Seonbulgajinsueorok」,which the Academy of Neo-humans and Cultural Archeology has Books of hidden secret,「濟衆甘露」, which Gyoujanggak, the number of the list:奎 19181, (Hanyang: Gyoujanggak, 1878).

Han Gang Hyen

Han Gang Hyen graduated from Gyeongsang National University, in the department of business administration, in Korea, from Mejiro(目白) University, in Japan, in the department of the comparing of language culture for 4 years, and from Mejiro(目白) University graduate school in the department of the international exchange cross- cultural study. He has worked as a director of the Korean New Religion Academy, still studies focusing on the predicitons of neohumans culture for dozens. He is a founding member of the International Academy of Neohumans Culture, chairperson in the future department and the general manager of the Academy, and wrote 『 The Secret of New Heaven.

The Final Issue of NRMs in the World
A Study for The Victory Altar & The Hidden Manna of New Heaven

Copyright : 2013 ⓒ GeumSeong Publishing Company & Han Gang- Hyen
Address : 49 Angok Street No205 Ave Sosa-gu
　　　　　Bucheon-si Kyeonggi-do, Korea

Tel : (+82)32-342-8774
Fax ; (+82)32-342-4367

Date of Publishing : 29 January 2014
ISBN : 978-89-967889-8-0
Price : US $21(21,000원)
Book Design : Wisdom of One Tree

www.ingramcontent.com/pod-product-compliance
Lightning Source LLC
Chambersburg PA
CBHW041432300426
44117CB00001B/3